When Nothing Feels Right at Thirty Five

A Mid-thirty Mental Meltdown and Faith Memoirs

Kring July

Amazon Kindle Direct Publishing

Copyright © 2021 Kresia Julio

All rights reserved

This book is memoir. It reflects the author's present recollections of experiences over time. No names have been changed, no characters invented, no events fabricated. The advice and notes found within may not be suitable for every situation. This work is sold with the understanding that neither the author nor the publisher are held responsible for the results accrued from the advice in this book.

No part of this book may be reproduced, or stored in a retrieval system, or transmitted in any form or by any means, electronic, mechanical, photocopying, recording, or otherwise, without express written permission of the publisher.

For more information, email: kringdzulai@gmail.com

Cover design by: Kring July

For my mom, Sepen,
Who has inspired my life's story.

For my brother, Gigil,
Who supported most of my crazy ideas.

For my husband, July,
Who is the superman behind.

For my toddler, Unyara,
Who motivated me to be the mother I never had.

For my cousins, Velou and Thelma,
Who were patient and understood my moods.

For my family and friends,
Who gave me encouragement to chase my dream.

And for my Savior, Jesus,
Who is relentless in His love and forgiveness and
always guiding me through all my life's stories.

CONTENTS

Title Page

Copyright

Dedication

Preface

Pre-Birthday Meltdowns — 1

Chapter One-Behind the Superwoman — 19

Chapter Two-To the Friends, I've Loved and Lost — 30

Chapter Three–The Curse of the Eldest Child — 40

Chapter Four–Managing Self-Sabotage — 54

Chapter Five-Here Comes Motherhood — 66

Chapter Six — The Wanderfull Life — 77

Chapter Seven–Hooked on a Fitness — 92

Chapter Eight — Faith in the Thirties — 101

Chapter Nine — Life of Faith — 122

Chapter Ten– Product of Faith — 136

Epilogue — 171

| Acknowledgement | 173 |
| About The Author | 179 |

PREFACE

I've been writing since time immemorial. Maybe I haven't improved my skills because I only love to write about myself. I'm not that talkative before. I have a hard time telling feelings to people. It just doesn't feel safe to tell my seatmate that I got a crush on the bully guy. Trust is always an issue. So I kept my secrets in my notes. Then one day, I saw a friend with a Filipino pocketbook. I don't like her that much, but I forced myself to be friends with her because she had something I like. After reading a couple of them at home under the blanket, they inspired me to write my own. I've written a couple. Just imagine all my pink class notes full of scribbles. I wanted to try my luck and have them published. Unfortunately, I failed because I would have forced you to read the fruits of my craziness if I didn't. Writing a book and have it published is on my bucket list. I wonder if I will achieve that. Let's just wait and see.

Above is an excerpt from the tons of posts that I have on my 12-year-old blog. I wrote it back in 2012. I'm just happy that I have the bravery to chase my dream of publishing my book now. And I think I have only changed a little. My favorite topic is still myself. The difference is that I understand why I love myself this time.

This book tells about the stories of transition from my Godless twenties down to my faith-filled thirties. From the stories of my birth 35 years ago, the crisis in my twenties, and the latest crisis in my thirties. My journey of how I broke free from the pains of my childhood through faith and achieved a 65% life fulfilment at 35.

"When Nothing Feels Right at 35!" is an answer to the dreaded feeling of a mid-thirty turmoil, hoping to one day read this book when I'm 45 and laughed at how mental I was at 35. It is a story of self to God-confidence, pains turned to gains, tests turned testimonies. A story of chasing the fulfilled life despite the struggles of constant self-sabotage and mental crisis. This book is a testimony of how a relationship with Christ can change everything.

This Is How It Started.

Feeling the weight of the mid-30 crisis since 2021 started, I wanted to get busy with back-to-back activities for my upcoming 35th birthday. However, after scheduling weekly activities in August with different friends to celebrate, the rising cases of Covid Delta got me worried. It was so hard to cancel, as I thought of my friend's disappointments. However, I didn't want to dishonor God for disobeying pleas to stay at home. I just feel extra down this year, and the thought that I'll be 35 and have done nothing great with my life is so strong.

I was super down after canceling all the plans. In one of my morning times with God, the idea of writing a book surfaced. Initially ignored it, but it was so strong and kept on popping up. God sends breadcrumbs that the book might just be what I needed to save me from a total mental meltdown.

When I realized it might be God's lead, on July 25, I created a book plan—created my autobiography with titles that I would want to write about. After the titles, I researched writing a book and the target word count. When I had the word count, I set daily targets. The initial target was 2k words/day.

I was having second thoughts of sharing about the plan to write a book. However, the first four days of writing were fun. Knowing I have a target to write a 2k word article a day after my office hours helped me stop the urge to overwork. It was easy to prioritize the tasks at work, so I can go offline by 8M and start writing by 9 PM after dinner. I spent 2 hours every night. I spent most of the weekends writing and reading about self-publishing. I have learned a lot while doing this passion project. In my first week, the experiences make me fulfilled already.

God's constant guidance and newfound fulfillment gave me the bravery to post about the book on the first day of my birth month. I was a little sad that only 5 of my FB friends reacted to the announcement. However, unlike the previous me, I knew better. Besides, I am not doing it for people but myself.

On July 31, I made it to 15K words after a week of writing. 26k words by August 6. On August 10, I made it to 40k and revealed the cover of the book. The cover page is an actual photo of my first Psoriasis episode on October 29, 2020, which was mentioned in the book, too. With four more days until the writing deadline on August 14, I felt the book was complete at 40K words. Book polishing started on August 11 and continues until the book release on August 20. The plan is to self-published it on both channels: Digital and Paperback. Connect with me through: WNFRat35.wordpress.com

PRE-BIRTHDAY MELTDOWNS

Every year since I have had the opportunity of celebrating and thinking about my life, the days before my birth month are the craziest. My brain goes into overdrive. Thoughts of things that I should do to commemorate the last few moments of the existing age are overwhelming. Days ago, I contemplated erasing all my social media existence and just moved out of the spotlight. I am not a celebrity, but a shameful admission of delusions being one. But of course, I still love the spotlight. Going on full offline mode is impossible, despite the increased self-scrutiny and guilt because of my social media habits since becoming a born-again Christian. I still think that social media is a splendid avenue to spread some love and, when I allow myself to, occasionally send bad vibes to the people who said I wouldn't amount to anything because of my Mom. Despite the things that God has blessed me with, thoughts about my mom still have the power to bring me down. I understand how she became a teenage mom who attracted guys for money and mistreated her kids for apparently no reason. However, the mark and the pain it caused are so deep that complete healing is still unreachable. Mom's diagnosis of Bipolar Disorder in twenty-seventeen didn't change things. It was a revelation but, there were mixed emotions.

It felt liberating to have this part of me out. I rarely highlight the "negative side" as they are too dark and don't match the reformed me. Giving in to the dark is no longer a habit, unlike in twenty-eleven when I had my first major mental meltdown — the mid-twenty crises. I am not confident if mental health was already a thing then, but I wouldn't know. It seems I just woke up after years of self-absorption. Not listening very well with others seemed to be my thing, plus a regular pattern of pre-birthday mental meltdowns.

The triggers of the mental meltdown are still somewhat unknown. However, when the effects are out, I usually step in to prevent a full-blown "mental stress" that may cause a second "Psoriasis" episode. Twenty-twenty was crazy because of Psoriasis. The signs usually start day by day when the darkness just crept in little by little, attaching negativity to any words I received. As "words" are my love language, I value others' words about me a lot, especially those I invited into my vulnerability. When my husband casually commented how I had been "crazier" in the passing months, and he expected it as a yearly pre-birthday mental meltdown, it drove me to the edge. I have high respect and love for my husband.

Instead of scowling right away, I started pondering on what he said. It drove me to revisit my life blog and searched for the word "crisis." Oh dear, yes, you guessed it. The shreds of evidence are all in the blog. Every year, starting my mid-twenty crises, April to July's posts were very disturbing. I was only thinking about the challenge of celebrating my birthdays, doing it differently, and throwing myself a surprise to remember the new age, unaware that if I don't, my vengeful self will be out to get me. Thirty-five is a big deal. That is why I scheduled an entire month of celebration, but because of Covid-19 Delta, I canceled everything. Imagine the wrath of my vengeful self. But what can I do? The pandemic is much, much scarier now at this wave. My heart would break every time I can read stuff from my messenger.

Another thing to thank with this mental meltdown is the push to have social rest. And, unlike the twenty-five-year-old version of me, my soon-to-be-thirty-five-year-old version had Jesus. I understand that when good doesn't happen, it only means that God is cooking something better. And so, I went to my nook and, thanks to God's leading, drafted my debut book. This book that you are reading now. When nothing feels right at thirty-five, what should you do? You write a book. Anyway, I don't know if I'll have the energy to turn this into my debut book because ENFJs (Extraverted, Intuitive, Feeling, Judging) from Myers-Briggs Personality Type has weaknesses such as unrealistic and overly idealistic. Only God knows if I can cover what I set out to do for this book, but regardless of what will happen, I'm holding on to one thing — God always has the best plan. Besides God's purpose, I also needed this book to stop myself from a mid-forty crisis in twenty-thirty-one. Sadly, we found out that my aunt has schizophrenia at twenty-fifteen, followed by my mom with bipolar in twenty-seventeen. However, I am always grateful to God because He always guides me to turn my tests into testimonies, and my pains into gains. I'm unsure if writing the book can stop the looming psoriasis episode. However, I'm confident that it will keep my mind away from the stress. The cover was during my first Psoriasis episode. I remembered how crazy that was. While suffering from psoriasis, thoughts that can affect my brain are constant.

Publish a book or become a YouTube influencer with a thousand followers, enough to monetize by forty. Close all my social media and go dark until I figure out what I want to do with my life. Start a new blog, "Paint Me A Forty," narrating how I'm feeling at thirty-four with less than six years left before my life starts in "Life starts at Forty." And oh, before I forget, my Psoriasis would have celebrated its six-year birthday by then too.

My brain has been in constant overdrive, which makes me somehow baffled, as I don't think Psoriasis has anything to do with it. I am angry about almost everything. The only thing that can somehow appease the continuous flow of trashy thoughts is reading my Bible app story and a plan on "healing." My day always starts with the Bible app story, but little things tick me off like a bomb. I was healing continuously outside, albeit slowly, but better than nothing. However, my feelings keep magnifying everything.

My daughter's minder's social media habits rarely annoy me, but during the episode, I just always notice her on the phone chatting instead of playing with my two-year-old toddler. I don't know if that's the case or my brain is just doing the tricks. It came to a point where I started thinking of just letting her go if the only thing that she can do was laundry and cooking, which I can outsource as needed. I also noticed how my husband scrolls endlessly on his news feed and seems to care more about other people's lives than our own. I also see that if I don't do things on my own, nothing gets done. Not only that, but I must also demand everything.

"Where Do I Go from Here Thoughts" is common like clockwork. I was pondering on becoming a YouTube influencer. For all the years that I have been blogging or writing about my life, it is the first time I want to make money out of my passion. It is out of this world, considering everything that is going on in my life. If there's a mid-thirty crisis, that's maybe the phase that I'm going through. I feel stuck in a loop of the ultimate mundane, as if I'm a hamster on a wheel. I'm running but not going anywhere. At thirty-four, I'm terrified that it is all that I will ever be. The current conditions were not bad but losing the energy to push and settle was.

I felt it would be better not to write about shameful feelings. Yet somewhere in my subconscious, I am urged to because, these feelings will be a nugget of wisdom, like the mid-twenty crisis posts that make me all warm inside when revisited. These feelings seem wrong, but what I will do from here on, responding to all the overdrives, is essential. And as I was writing, I realized that what I do to react to this feeling doesn't matter, providing I know the root cause of all the commotions in my head. Is this all true? Or is there a chance that Psoriasis has somehow turned the nudge higher for every aspect of my system, not just the physical but mental too? Scary, but God knows. On a side note, further introspective leads me to deduct that this feeling has been hanging way before Psoriasis, especially the falling out of social media love. I'm terrified of becoming a total social media addict.

I spend most of my time admiring or judging other people instead of focusing on my own, and my habits have been lukewarm over the passing years. Not only that, I have cleaned up my friend's list several times and thought of deactivating for good. My recent adjustments were removing my Instagram followers for those I haven't interacted with within three months. I have also removed all notifications, including messenger, so it doesn't interrupt my day. I only check sporadically. Likewise, I don't know if all the things I have written make sense or are valid, but I know that writing them frees my mind from the burden. Maybe it's not psoriasis, but only God knows what will happen from here on. Where do I go from here?

It took me twenty-five days to write about how I felt when I knew I had psoriasis. By that time, my forehead is free from lesions. Thankfully, unlike the first week, I already have days when I woke up feeling good. I will never forget the twenty-ninth of September, twenty-twenty, as another day that changed my life.

Psoriasis is a stable, noncontagious autoimmune disease characterized by raised areas of abnormal skin. These areas are typically red or purple on people with darker skin, dry, itchy, and scaly. Psoriasis varies in severity from small, localized patches to complete body coverage.

I posted about Psoriasis on my life blog, *lifewithkring.wordpress.com*. Eventually, I created a separate blog about it in *lifewithpsor.wordpress.com*. I didn't share it immediately on my social media channels for various reasons. I don't want anyone pitying me because of psoriasis. The timing was not right, and I was not ready to decline recommendations on a probable psoriasis remedy. However, despite my initial hesitations, I know that Psoriasis happened to me for a reason. God never gave me something too hard to handle. Once He does, almost always, He wants me to inspire and glorify His name by sharing about it, just like His miracle of giving me my firstborn despite polycystic ovarian syndrome since twenty-ten.

Because by documenting my experiences, I will remember that even if psoriasis is impossible to heal, God made it disappear. Aside from that, sharing gives me hope of finding people who can collaborate in spreading awareness about the condition. Writing about my journey has helped me during that episode. However, God was remarkable. By Christmas of twenty-twenty, I'm free of all skin lesions. Whenever I think that Psoriasis is a lifelong disease, see posts of others who have it worse, I can't help but feel worried. But during that event, God was there. The revelation took a blow but my faith was more robust than the worry. The constant prayers that the first psoriasis episode will become a part of a memory one day too was answered. I am so thankful to God because the lesions have reacted well to the topical medications. Proceeding to the costly treatment would have been crazy.

According to an online source, the typical out-of-pocket costs for Psoriasis treatment in the United States for patients covered by health insurance, typically consist of doctor visit copays, prescription drug copays of $5 to $50 or more, or coinsurance of 10% to 50% -- which can reach $500 or more for certain drugs. According to the National Psoriasis Foundation, copays for phototherapy can be $50 or more per session. Treatment for psoriasis typically is covered by insurance, but certain medications might not be covered in some cases. For example, biologic therapies for psoriasis states that some medications are covered only when certain criteria are met, including other treatments having failed.

Psoriasis treatment typically costs about $2,000 to $6,000 or more for phototherapy -- or up to $11,000 for initial treatment, then $1,000 to $2,000 per month afterward, for newer biologic medications. For example, the national average cost per session for phototherapy is about $63, with a total of $3,780 or more for a typical 30 weeks of twice weekly treatment. Or some patients buy a home unit for about $2,000 to $6,000 or more. $1,900 for a one-month supply of syringes filled with the biologic. A specific type would cost $11,400 total for the first three months of treat-

ment, then $1,900 per month afterward. Biologics might be used in severe, debilitating cases that have not responded to other treatments.

One of the major triggers of Psoriasis is stress but knowing the expensive treatment would give you more stress. That is what happen to me. On my first checkup with Psoriasis, the dermatologist directly discussed about biologics, mentioning thousands of pesos. It scared me and give me more lesions.

My first Psoriasis episode was the longest check up marathon for me who hated medical check ups. Five different doctors in a span of two weeks. If there's another thing to thank in this quarantine, it is, appreciating the rise of telemedicine. Without it, for sure, the already delayed check ups would be delayed further as we all know, going to a check up is such a pain. The waiting sucks the life out of you.

Before I proceed to the five doctors, let me tell you first how I have survived the two months of dandruff thinking it was caused by polycystic ovarian syndrome. Since Unyara's birth in October twenty-eighteen, my menstruation has been absent. It just got back in January twenty-twenty. However, it was absent again until May twenty-twenty, so I suspected that my polycystic ovarian syndrome is back.

Because of Covid-19, visiting the obstetrician was far from my mind. Besides, I kind of lost hope in managing my polycystic ovarian syndrome too. The dandruff was clearing up after applying the home remedies for Seborrheic Dermatitis, so I was prepared to ignore the husband's reminder to have my dandruff checked. But after some time, the skin problem reached my forehead then to my neck then eventually to my back and my groins. The husband was now frantic with how lightly I am still taking things. Because I am practicing being a submissive wife, I reluctantly checked the options for check up. The husband raised the concern in on the last day of July, but it took me two months to schedule my first teleconsult on the twenty-sixth of September.

After a week of on and off searching on how to telemedicine using insurance without a phone to get an Letter of Authorization from the insurance, I got frustrated and proceeded to have a personal paid checkup on the twenty-sixth of September. My complains were the absent of menstruation since May twenty-twenty, dandruff, back & groins allergy with shoulder and leg pains. Diagnosis was muscle pains due to breastfeeding and concur with polycystic Seborrheic Dermatitis. The prescriptions pain killer and requested to have my polycystic checked by an obstetrician.

Two days after my first Doctor checkup, I had my first "itch" attack on the twenty-eight of September. It was so annoying that despite the fear and hesitations of going out for fear of Covid-19, I had to stomach going to the nearest hospital after not finding an obstetrician in telemedicine. Without a second thought, I decided to visit, only to find out how the processes changed due to Covid-19. However, God is awesome. Despite the change of processes, I was still able to do a checkup even if I didn't have an appointment for that day.

Sharing the same complains, the obstetrician requested for transvaginal ultrasound and pap smear. As she was checking my cervix for abnormalities, she saw my groins and advised me to visit a derma as it looks like I have Psoriasis. When I hear it, I felt down as on my research, Seborrheic Dermatitis is better than Psoriasis. My obstetrician must have felt my fear, so she later explained that Psoriasis can be managed and that I shouldn't be stressed as stress is a Psoriasis trigger.

I took the advice of my obstetrician. I had my allergies checked by a dermatologist. Unfortunately, the first dermatologist that checked me directly advised for the expensive treatment. I was stressed more. Thankfully, the husband stepped in and told me to have a second opinion. By this time, I made sure I have a dermatologist that is covered by our insurance. She was so nice and supportive of the entire process.

After a month of knowing that the allergies were

caused by Psoriasis and, two derma prescriptions, the Psoriasis in my groins and neck were healed. The back and face lesions were improved. Although the scalp wasn't given any medication, the flakes has become less and less. There was no major "itch" attack anymore as when I start to feel itchy, I quickly revert my thoughts into something positive. It really helps that I know how the stress could increase the itch. Knowing that the medications are just there to mitigate, I was more careful with my emotions. I was looking into diet and strengthening my spiritual health more as it can help combat with the main trigger – STRESS. Every day is a day of learning. I'm also reading a lot of healing bible plans to motivate me on the journey. Because of that first Psoriasis episode, I have become more attuned with the bodily indications of an upcoming Psoriasis attack. Judging how I'm feeling nowadays, the stress threatened another Psoriasis setback. The stress is mostly from work and the feelings of not being enough at thirty-five. However, unlike in twenty-twenty, despite the fear of psoriasis, I am letting go and letting God.

Going back, why should you read this book when it's just a bunch of monologues from a nobody who is probably crazy but not clinically diagnosed? I won't promise anything. As someone who takes words as actions, which is one of the most common reasons for the husband and I's disagreements, I won't say more. I don't want to build any hopes about this book. I was only writing my heart out for this introduction and planned to merge some thoughts from my twelve-year-old blog.

I have been blogging since twenty-o-nine on WordPress, but I'm pretty sure I have an early one made in twenty-o-seven because that's when I started my first job. Before work, all my thoughts were in a diary or a random notebook.

There are tons of excuse why I shouldn't write a book, aside from people may not be interested to read it, but I focused on my childhood dream to have my own published book. I was so obsessed with my dream that my mom, who could barely feed two mouths, gave me a typewriter when I graduated from elementary school. At thirteen, I barely understood how hard it was for mom to produce the gift. The gift only made sense now.

> "You never know how much your mom loved you until you have a child to love."

Understanding my mom was not my best asset. Growing up in a neighborhood that treated her like trash made me think I am trash. However, the child is not a reflection of the parent. Happiness and success are possible, despite how dark our starting points are. Mom was a teenage mom at seventeen going on eighteen, as I was born on the twentieth of August nineteen-eighty-six, less than two months away from her birthday. Had I been born after her birthday on the seventh of October, it would have been slightly okay, as she could declare that she was of legal age. On the year Mom celebrated her thirty-fifth birthday, I was already seventeen years old and in my first year in college. I couldn't help but compare Mom to how I am now at thirty-five. Our circumstances are unique. Her age when she had me was seventeen, while I had Unyara, my firstborn, almost twice her age when she had me. Bringing a child into the world in my thirties is not a plan. My complicated experience with her caused most of it.

At seventeen, when I started college, I had a strained relationship with Mom. We used to be the best of friends, but somehow it took a wrong turn during my college years. Despite our strained relationship, like the typewriter graduation gift, I wondered how she afforded a whole roasted pork for my eighteenth birthday. We were destitute. There was no party and dancing, but the roasted pork was something. Now, as I'm at the same age as my Mom was when I was seventeen, with her unstable income, my respect for her grew as I realized how hard it was to earn money. If things were different now and without her bipolar disorder, I would certainly enjoy talking to her about how opposite our circumstances are at thirty-five.

To celebrate my mid-thirties, writing a book is

a celebration of both my birth and the woman behind it all. I have a highly complex relationship with Mom. I wonder if I can put all the complications into a single book, would it become a guidebook to those who are in the same boat? At thirty-five, I can now appreciate the "like mother, like daughter" quote. But when I was growing up, especially during my adolescent years, this has been my constant source of pain. My mom hasn't been an excellent role model, with her reputation of having two kids out of wedlock and her closeness with men. And although I'm certain that being emotionally unstable is partly a choice, through the years that I have had this pre-birthday meltdown, this is the first that I have accepted that IT'S OKAY NOT TO BE OKAY.

As a teenager, whenever I watched a local television show, "Maala-ala Mo Kaya," back in high school, I would often dream of sending my story as it seemed more exciting and tear-jerking than some episodes. Of course, I never had the courage that time, and, back in high school, I was still very insecure about my background and often felt like an outcast. The life that I have lived was not a bed of roses. It's only by the grace of God that I can write an entire book of notes to myself. Experiencing a mental meltdown is difficult, but unlike my twenties, I am more equipped to handle the crisis now.

Throughout the book, I will mention the mid-thirty crises. To understand the feelings, you can look them up on Google for more context. I sometimes have this bout of depressive and manic states, which my husband relates to bipolar, but I'm confident this feeling is not that. Per definition from various online sources, midlife crisis symptoms vary widely from person to person. The most common midlife crisis age range is thirty-five to fifty-five, with variability between genders. There's an overlap between many symptoms of a midlife crisis and depression. Figuring out what's going on can be a challenge, as different disorders may occur at once. Feeling disappointed in life, intense feelings of nostalgia, and chronic reminiscence about the past are early symptoms. Then it can escalate to feelings of boredom, emptiness, meaninglessness, impulsive, often rash action, and dramatic changes in behavior and appearance. If not detected early, it can even result in permanent damage like marital infidelity or constant thoughts about cheating, constantly comparing oneself to others who seem happier or more fulfilled, and intense feelings of regret.

From the above symptoms, thankfully, I didn't get to the permanent damage. My daily connection with God has helped me sort out the feelings. It's crazy, but it is possible. I'm writing a book to take my mind away from the crisis and help others who experience the same. Coping up with this crisis is critical, as it will surely propel how life turns out for the next ten years. Let this be the only hasty decision that I will make. I need to talk to my husband and those closest to me about what I am experiencing to help me reach reality. I need to be kind to myself and others.

If you pick this book because you have experienced the same, please remember not to worry and overthink. So, while this book is primarily a note to self, I pray that this book could be an inspiration for you, too. May my pains that have turned to purpose, my tests that have turned to testimonies, and all the little details of my life that have made me who I am today be your inspiration. Press forward in whatever season that you are in life now. We all have many roles to play. It takes a specific strength to balance them all. Do not do anything on your own! Look for a source of power that will never run out. Let Jesus find you. Whatever your circumstances now, know that you got this! Thank you for diligently finishing my introduction. And while I can only pray that this book can add value to your life, connect with me through this book's Instagram: WNFRat35. I won't mind, even if you just read the title or made it through my introduction. Thank you so much!

CHAPTER ONE–BEHIND THE SUPERWOMAN

When Unyara was born in twenty-eighteen, my eldest, although she is an only child in twenty-twenty-one as I drafted this book, the husband and I are not closing our door for a blessing. Hello there, second child, if you are reading this in the future. The book starts with the story of the woman behind — My Mom! As I brainstormed how to do this chapter, I received an excellent idea: skim all my blog posts and check the write-ups with "Mom" on them. As of writing, I have a thousand and two hundred published posts. Yeah, I have a sea of thoughts in the blog, so why not use some, right?

There were eighty-nine posts from the results. And as expected, every year has a representative, but most of the writing was from twenty-eleven when I had my mid-twenty crises. It is not a surprise as even though I have already moved on from the belief that our parents have anything to do with who we are, it is undeniable that my Mom was my "kryptonite." Beyond the facade of strength, all of it would melt if you expose me to my Mom, especially before she had her myoma operation in twenty-fourteen. She is just vicious and abusive. All she wants is money, and I was like a walking money machine, especially when I started working at twenty-o-seven.

In my elementary years, I would often create a fantasy to justify Mom's cruelty. I would imagine that my mom only adopted my brother and me. Given our "rich kid" physique, we are heirs and heiresses kidnapped from our home because our actual parents were mean to Mom. I can't recall how many times I plan to escape and ride a random boat to Manila. Find our birth parents because I was so confident that no mother can do the things, she did with us, especially to me. She broke me beyond repair. It made me feel less of myself, unlovable, and a burden. There are still skeletons in the closet with everything I have shared about her cruelty. It is still hard to understand, but when I received Jesus in June of twenty-seventeen, He melted my pains and made a new person out of the ashes of the brokenness. I have forgiven Mom, but of course, I never forgot the pains.

Thirty-five years ago, I was born out of wedlock. It was challenging for an only child. With another one, it was harsh. Mom had me two months before turning eighteen, a critical age for women. Mom lost the chance to enjoy the period of freedom by keeping me. Many times, in the past, I wished Mom didn't. I have experienced so much pain because she saved me. To be alive and barely living? It was a curse. Dying was my constant prayer.

At an early age, my life was a constant roller coaster ride. At three, Mom left Dad, tagging my newborn brother, which I often considered a bother. Mom went to work faraway before I could celebrate the feeling of no belt pains and sack smoke punishment from our old home. I was alone and scared. In Mom's absence, I noticed how our new home differs from our old one. I was the only kid in the house. And the usual ploy that earned me slaps and pinches in the old house seemed to amuse the new. Tears that gave me pain from the past made me new toys in the present. They all adored me. The feeling was strange but lovely. For the first time, I feel loved and accepted.

From being shy and aloof, I became everybody's favorite. My natural wit and brilliance make me especially drawn to learn things quickly. The days become months and then years. I have forgotten about Mom and that feeling of being unwanted and a burden. With Grandma, Aunties, and Uncles, I am the star. And I thought I would never feel those horrible feelings again. I was wrong. On my first-grade commencement, Mom returned after around four years of working. She was so happy to see what became of the child she left years ago. Because my uncle's family has grown to three kids, it was harder for my brother and me to share the spotlight. Mom had no choice. She had to pick up the role that she left off, a role, later learned, should have been forgotten. Little brother is now four — a year older than I was when we left Dad. He didn't recognize Mom at all and seemed uninterested to know her. In Mom's effort to reconnect and make up for the lost times, she pulled us away from the happy home and the people we've learned to love. In doing so, she had to work double to support us both.

Mom becomes everything. Fridays saw her selling at the cockpit. Other days, she roamed house to house for manicures and pedicures. Another three years passed; Mom decided she needed to come back to work. And with that came a revelation. I was not a child of Dad, but another. A man Mom is also in a relationship with during the time I was conceived. A revelation not thoroughly explained to a ten-year-old. I grew up confused and doubting the truth about how I came to be — it was then that the unwanted feeling haunts me again. In my pain, Grandma was my strength. Mom had become so consumed with feeding us that she had become more bitter and cranky. Slight misgivings will not go unnoticed. My happy and carefree life turned into a hell of torture again. This time, I shared it with my little brother. Mom prohibited us from playing with neighbors. Sibling bickering was a mortal sin. And because Mom saw a future in my intelligence, she didn't falter in pushing me to the top. And when I lose my guard in rare moments, she is quick to whip me back on track.

I remember a time in grade three when I got zero on a three-point exam. The lesson was about synonyms, but the sneaky teacher gave us an antonym exam. Because of my carelessness and pride, I never listened to the whole instruction. It was probably the first "itlog" of my life. I was so scared that it would reach my Mom that I had to ask our neighbors not to tell her. Unfortunately, as I'm very ill-mannered during my elementary years, most neighbors who were my classmates hate me. At lunch, when I went home, Mom had to stop doing laundry and almost beat me to death. A classmate tells my Mom during lunchtime that I got zero on our exam. I cursed that classmate growing up. I also learned not to be zero and always listen to the instructions first.

Despite how good I am in school, it was never good enough for Mom. The torture continues. Then grandma died. My only consolation and hope die with it. With grandma gone, my world turned into an abyss of pain. But maybe because I was always a favored child of God, my unmarried uncle is fast to fill in grandma's void. Then the baby sister came. I was so angry and ashamed. Mom didn't learn at all. Despite the struggles, she still has the heart to bring another human into the world. Mom was twenty-seven. I realized she was still very young then. As we got to know the baby sister, I realized she was not a bother at all. Baby sister taught me how to care for a newborn. The new Dad's presence was frequent. But as the months turned to years, he once again, vanished. I later learned his story when I saw him again after six years as a teenager. Until now, Mom is still unsure who my dad is. Though I don't know who my dad is among the two men in Mom's life, I am content knowing that I have two dads. It has its perks. The only thing I am sure of is that my baby brother and baby sister don't have the same dad.

Because life was harsh, and the new dad left, Mom gave up baby sister for adoption. The once horror house turned to heaven when she came, so the thought of giving her away took a blow. But Mom always has the last say. She gave her away. The months that followed were cruel. Mom succumbs to her bad habits of liquor and drugs. With every drunk moment, little brother's and mine's screams of agony always fill the air. It was then that I thought of dying to escape. And if only drinking the water from a mosquito repellant could kill, I wouldn't have been alive to share this story. Nature made diamonds from too much pressure, like how my pains made me who I am! I couldn't count how many times I tried killing myself, running away from home, and so on. The thought of our survival always humbles my brother and me. We didn't survive, but we went beyond. Now, our cranky Mom is no longer a crank but with pride for her two children, who finished a degree with her meager means until twenty-seventeen on the onset of her bipolar disorder. Our childhood has shaped us. Between eating nothing, rice, and salt, I vowed to do what I can to succeed. Dreams are not the ones I have in my sleep but fueled my very existence. And though I am thankful because we are not who our parents are, it is still not entirely true. Reading back at my first digital post dedicated to my Mom on twenty-o-nine, I'm just grateful that I'm still alive and thriving despite all the pains.

It was a crazy experience, our first time riding a dump truck on our own. I remembered how I kept praying for safety as I tell stories to the driver and the truck boy. However, the ride back was not our only problem. The silence at Plaza while walking in the middle of the street before seeing a taxi terrified us. After that ordeal, I cursed family gatherings. I favored celebrating birthdays with friends rather than with family. Aside from that crazy experience, I don't feel well around my family because I cannot act according to what I want, especially around my Mom. I always need to calculate my every move to keep her happy. It's so tiresome and stressful. My hesitation to celebrate birthdays with my family was more of a preference, but through the years, it was the only thing that kept me alive — being away from the toxicity of my family life.

If I was nice to myself, I should have fled from my venomous mom. I often wonder if other moms are just as devilish. However, the good side reasoned that wicked ways for a mom are maybe common. It has always been my prayer for mom's evil ways to vanish and that if I continue being nice and submit to her demands, she will change. But as the years passed, the ill part overpowers the good side of me. That part tells me I'm a fool for believing goody's reason. I should no longer let goody talk me into something unnecessary. I should not let my mom manipulate me by her wicked ways. She had done it many times already. What happened should remind me that even if I gave my whole life to her, she would still remain an ungrateful, devilish mom who never thinks of anything but herself. I was jealous of others for having a normal mom. I wonder what it feels like to have one. My mom gave me the creeps of having my child. Terrified that I can never be a wonderful mom to my children, or worse, I could never be a good wife to my husband because of how badly she raised me. I hated men because of the trauma. Because of hatred, I can't remember how many times I have prayed for her to die. The Pinoy saying "Masamang damo, matagal mamatay!" through the years has become a usual line. But when she had a near-death experience in twenty-fourteen during her myoma operation, I realized that despite the hate, the thought of her death is still painful.

Thirty-five years ago, life was hard for my Mom. A "teen" forced into adulthood. Not the typical Mom, the sweet and caring one, but no matter how I try to separate myself from her, I realized that I am indeed my mother's daughter. Beyond the hurts, I also remember a time when Mom and I used to be buddies. I tell her everything. Over dinner, I usually recall what happened to me the entire day in high school. I tell her how I caught one of my classmates staring at me the whole Social Studies class in my third year at my new high school. Or how my teacher hated me for overpowering her voice with my giggles. Mom always listened with fondness and pride in her eyes. When she doesn't like something, I did in my story, she'd usually reprimand me. I'll make sure I'd never make the same mistake Mom pointed out. On weekends, I used to go with Mom to her home services. Listening to her brag about me is nothing new. Mom is proud of me. Once, I saw a worn picture of my brother and me in her pocket. I was sure she used it to brag about us.

Come college, our rift started when I found someone. I never talked to Mom that much anymore. She was jealous. Mom and I have never been the same since. There was a time that I hated her so much that I often prayed she would die so that I could live my life free of her. Who needs a mother like her, anyway? She was that vicious mom who deliberately makes me suffer by getting all my scholar allowance and leaving me with almost nothing. She didn't die. Thank God. Maybe I didn't pray about it earnestly. When asked to describe her, I usually said she's unusual. Mom used to force my brother and me to discos. Mom loves to disco herself. She was so friendly, a total crowd-pleaser. My brother and I hated it. She is appreciative of other kids but made our life a living hell. She would punish us with every minor mistake. I ran away from home a lot when I was in elementary school. Mom is usually good, but beware when she's drunk, she's a total devil. That's why we always hate it when she drinks alcohol. Even though she's changed now, my brother and I still resented her drinking because we would remember the past.

The most memorable memory was when my brother and I hid under the table. Whenever Mom is alcohol drunk, she would punish us. In her anger, knowing that we were hiding, she took a bolo and chopped the round table away with us under it. There were so many "near-death" moments in Mom's hands from my childhood that I often wonder how on earth did we survive from all those. My brother and I are true survivors for becoming who we are today. Though we still remember our hate, we could never deny the significant impact on our lives. True, she's not the perfect Mom, but I could never think of anyone who could to find the energy to keep a long-term friendship. There was a time during my twenties when I was so down that I thought of ranting to my heart's content. On impulse, I removed all the notifications from the blog, considering what the point is when I'm not sure if my friends are reading my updates. I added the reports to share with them what I'm doing. I'm not a call friend type. Not only that, but I also rarely ask a friend to go out to. Waiting to be needed and hating to ask for assistance are two of my friend traits. Though I often wonder why some have super friends, I'm complacent in knowing the cause. It would be nice for someone to drag me to coffee shops, then we can rant our hearts out. As I have a terrible experiences with group gatherings that ends up talking about other people, I always try to control the conversations. But I noticed how most people felt uncomfortable talking about themselves, so I always talked about myself to fill in the silence or sway it from the gossip. Talking about people not around gives me gossip alarm and makes me sick. Growing up in a small community where gossips are rampant, I hated it. I vowed that when I grow up, I shall not talk about other people unless necessary. My life has so many happenings that avoiding talking about other people is easy. It seemed it is not the case with others.

Even if there was someone I could rant my hurt out in my twenties, it never felt enough. I want girlfriends. Besides ranting, I longed to be surrounded by women who would lift me. Everything bores me. I hate to feel bored because if I do, I'll just remember how depressed I am. I am depressed and crazy. As much as possible, I want to avoid feeling anything but excitement. I think having girlfriends could help me forget my family problems especially my Mom's craziness.

Being in a room with Mom is a struggle. She'll just talk and talk like there's no tomorrow. The more I listened, the more unhappy I was. She's unbearable. She always is. Her sickness magnifies that viciousness, in the opposite direction. It annoys me so much.

I need a friend to share how I love my new hair. Probably, I need a funny one who will add energy to my otherwise dull life. I need someone to tell me I'm wrong and be transparent with her thoughts. My hair seems to project another side of me that my long hair didn't when I cut it very short for the first time in twenty-eleven. My short hair projects optimism and positivity. With my long hair, I remembered a feeling of innocence and submission. With this, I feel like I'm in control. Being a new employee excites me as well. It seems there's so much to learn. And it could be my chance to find my super friend too.

But I miss my elementary days when I only have one constant companion. I can't remember how our friendship started. For me, it's always been her & me. We're neighbors and classmates, so we are in each other's company all week. She is everything I'm not, kind, and diligent compared to me, who is harsh and lazy. The only thing I'm good at is studying. Because she's such a busy kid at home, she can't learn properly. I can't do anything but that. When I met her, I saw a new world. I wanted to be as good as her in cleaning, washing, and all the stuff that I can't do. I imitated her and tried hard to learn the things she can do. In return, I forced her to understand my ways, too. We graduated elementary, with me as Valedictorian and her, the first honorable. I wanted her to be Salutatorian to have scholarships and stick together in high school. God has other plans. I was devastated and afraid when she couldn't go with me to high school. I was never good at communicating with people, so I feared not having someone to listen to everything that I needed to say would hurt.

When I thought about her away for sure my world would eventually fall. It didn't. I learn to cope up with her absence. I try to reach out to others. But I could not create the same friendship in my new life. I was heartbroken. I badly want her back. God was so lovely that He made a way to fulfill that wish.

I transferred to her school by my third year in high school. I was all rainbows the heartbroken when we failed to reconnect. While I didn't find another, she has found a better me. And sadly, she doesn't want me anymore. I chased her around. I badly wanted her to remember who she was with me. All failed. From that time on, I vowed not to have anyone like her by my side anymore. She was my first heartbreak. Despite that, I have lots of things to thank her. What I am today would not be possible if she didn't help me mold a better me. If not for her, I would still be harsh and lazy, wrapped in my world and uncaring to the word, friend. Our short friendship started when we were ten and ended when we had separate high schools at thirteen. Time passed, and fast-forward to ten years ago. I was twenty-five. Sporadically, I wonder if I will be as open to others now if I had her to listen to all my woes. She was enough, and the need to grow out of my shell would have been useless. That separation from her was my first crisis.

The crisis with my best friend was the catalyst of my change into adolescence. Twelve years later from that crisis, I had my mid-twenty problems. It was the catalyst of my transformation into adulthood. Despite the years, I haven't moved on from our friendship. I compare every girl who becomes a friend with her. All of them fail. While I have so many now, there isn't a single constant one. No one knows all of me, from the dark to the fun to the reformed and the current version. But unlike before, I don't consider it wrong to have so many friends.

When I was in my mid-twenty crises, there wasn't anyone. My blog was my friend. I tell it about issues of my life that may not be an issue for me at twenty-five, but for others. Looking back at it, I'm thankful that I had captured that moment of my life in the blog because it's easier to put into the book. However, it would have been nice to have both. Through my pains, it is easier to appreciate what God has done in my life. I didn't know then that the hardships too shall pass. Twenty-five seems like a defining point of my existence. The choice that I make from that point has transformed my life. Now that I will be thirty-five, I can appreciate that I have not decided out of pressure. Despite not being in an intimate relationship with God then, He still guided me into His will. The pain points of my mid-twenty crisis seemed insignificant now that I am thirty-five. Praying that my pain points now at thirty-five will be negligible when I'm forty-five.

Compared to the mid-twenty version with no friends, I have tons now, but I still long for a tribe. A constant tribe where I would not outgrow because we have the same season. I don't have a problem finding connections with anyone, but keeping a tribe is hard. I may have changed over the years, but friendship is still a thing that is so hard.

At twenty-five, I was so confused about what I'm doing with my life. I wonder if the pains were light if I had a friend to share them. Everything seems entirely wrong. I feel caged and out of freedom. Much of the confusion comes from comparing with others and not communicating with my family about my feelings. At twenty-five, I see most people my age having the time of their life — traveling or getting focused on their significant others, while I'm drowning in family responsibilities. Instead of tapping me for a job well done, providing for the family, I felt like a victim of fate. And instead of doing something about it, like telling my family that I could not do the job forever and giving my brother a due date of when he will take over the responsibility, I remained silent about my sufferings. Get over it by staying away from what will make me compare, like spending so much time on social media. I focused on my goal to help the family and have become transparent that my help is not forever. Drawing the line and setting a deadline for the support has helped me find my direction.

I thought about doing a career shift too. To be a software engineer is not my dream. The pressures brought by it drove me nuts. After four years of working in a highly stressed industry, I thought I would have a stress-free life if I ended up being a teacher (no offense to teachers). I stayed because I realized that, yes, being a software engineer is crazy, but most of the pressures were not really about the job, but how I did the job. For the first four years, I didn't have any concept of work-life balance. When I transferred to my second job, it was then that I started seeing how outstanding it is to be working in Information Technology. The opportunities are endless. I have even worked abroad for six months.

At twenty-five, I was breaking and full of debt. It was tough to make ends meet when I started working, so debt has been my refuge. Like many others, I don't have any savings, but I had extras when my brother finally finished school. Instead of splurging it on things, I paid all my debts. I also set aside an amount for emergencies.

Being the eldest of a Filipino family, we can't just shrug off our family responsibilities, especially if we are our family's hope of survival. But we can manage our responsibilities by sharing the burden with the other family members. It took me a while to delegate and share the load because I thought I'm the only one who can. Eventually, when I saw my brother's success, I realized he could. We cannot change the family we came from, but we can change the family we will have. To my future family, I will set aside money for retirement and not succumb to the common practice of putting the burden on the eldest child. If I think I cannot provide, it's best not to have children at all.

When I wrote this, getting hitched was just an idea. Then things eventually started changing.

Three years after I wrote the pain points at twenty-five, I got engaged. We didn't have money savings, but we had mortgaged a condo. After our engagement, we had it rented out to save up for the wedding. Because we only had a year to prepare, we had an unconventional wedding to trim up the cost. I am beyond my pain points at twenty-eleven. It was the year that defined everything for me. And I thank God that I picked wisely with all the trials and the decisions that I had to choose. I am happy that God blessed me with a lot in my twenties. I may not have a constant friend, but God sent me too many. In my thirties, my goal is to let God lead me to the constants.

To all the friends that I loved and lost, I wonder if you ever remember our friendship. Despite the counts, I still remember you. In my thirties, I wish to share my pain points with a tribe. I am confident that this will make me better than I once was, but it would be exceptional to go through it with a support group.

At twenty-eleven, I had no one. Even God was leading me in the shadows. I basked in the glory of what, I thought, were personal achievements. This time I am better equipped. I have accepted that God made me for a purpose. Keeping my light on a single tribe is impossible. Besides, it is wrong to put your hopes on friendship when your first hope should be with God. I miss all the friends I have loved and lost, but I understand it is part of growing friendships. Writing this book has reminded me that friendships can only be achieve through God's leading and a fulfilled life through faith-filled Jesus-centered choices. Like love, friendship is also God's gift.

CHAPTER THREE– THE CURSE OF THE ELDEST CHILD

Introducing this book opens my complicated relationship with my Mom. Chapter one touches on how I came to be and the early childhood pains—chapter two talks about my most crisis, down to my first major one when I was twenty-five. Before sharing the rest of my situation, let's take a quick deep dive into why the problem happens to me. Why can't I be like ordinary people and treat life as they go? Creating circumstances that lead to a concern for me seemed to be a goal. Why am I prone to self-sabotage? Why do I feel trapped in patterns that create problems in my life and keep me from achieving my goals? Although I try to make changes and disrupt these patterns, somehow, I still end up in the same place, again and again.

Is this you? You may have the self-sabotaging pattern, as I do, too. Self-sabotage refers to behaviors or thought ways that hold you back and prevent you from doing what you want to do. It can be a combination of blaming others when things go wrong or choosing to walk away when things don't go smoothly. It can also be procrastination or picking fights with friends or partners. Dating people who aren't suitable for you or trouble stating your needs. Putting yourself down or believing you are not worthy of being loved.

According to various sources, self-sabotage happens when you do things adaptive in one context but are no longer necessary. These behaviors helped you adapt to a previous situation, like a traumatic childhood or toxic relationship, and survive the challenges you faced there. They may have soothed you or defended you, but these coping methods can cause difficulties when your situation changes. Here's a closer look at some significant contributing factors: patterns learned in childhood, past relationship dynamics, fear of failure, and a need for control.

Of all the years that I have tortured and self-sabotaged myself, twenty-twenty-ones' crisis was my first time acknowledging that something is wrong with me. I realized I am different from most people. However, it is thanks to the husband's patience and unconditional love that I can find time to take a pause, look inward, and hold on to my faith as my guide through all the sufferings.

> "If an outside force breaks an egg, life ends. If broken by inside force, life begins."

Twenty-twenty-one started on the wrong foot, especially at work. The good thing about life now is, although I am still broken, God is spectacular. Once I accepted salvation back in June of twenty-seventeen, Jesus's healing and love have provided comfort in my struggles. My dream of a fulfilled life is slowly becoming a reality. Despite the apparent lack of money growing up, cash and financial rewards did not motivate me. I have known that it might solve my problem, but having the lack of it has never pushed me to do anything.

This "no love for money" must be the reason that through my fourteen years at work, in my third company as of this writing, I have never experienced getting into a job through my desire and effort. All three just landed on my lap before or after a crisis. Way back when I wasn't a born-again Christian, I kept claiming that I was God's favorite for being ultra-blessed in many things. The word God's choice made more sense when Jesus happened to me on the third of June, twenty-seventeen. While my natural self-sabotage tendencies are outstanding, threatening my fulfillment of life, supernatural forces are always in the background to save me from myself.

The root causes of most of my crises are the coping patterns that I have learned from my childhood, the past relationship dynamics that I had growing up, the nagging fear of failure, and a need for control. It took me a while to realize that these root causes may stop my growth in my finances. But despite that, my heart is whole, knowing that my faith-filled choices have brought me this far. I may not be rich by the world's standards, broken and prone to self-sabotage but beyond blessed. There are things in my life that will always be a story to tell because Jesus made it all happen. Although, when it happened, I just saw it as a storm, but not the silver lining of God's purpose.

> *"The only time you should ever look back is to see how far you've come."*

My first job was on April twenty-o-seven. As part of the perks of graduating from a school that is the center of excellence in Information Technology and a government scholar, before we even graduate, companies would flock to our school for hiring. I was the lucky few who already have a job before getting a diploma. With just two weeks out of school, I started my first job in wide-eyed wonder, oblivious to the responsibility of being a first-time employee and the breadwinner of the family.

Thanks to my built-in tolerance of stress and hardships, despite the crazy experience of my first job, I became a regular employee. With the break-up from my four-year college sweetheart five months into the position, God blessed me despite the company-wide commotion for overreacting because of a broken heart through assumed betrayal and infidelity. Gosh! Talk about being young, dumb, broke, and stupidly in love! Ha!

Twenty-zero-seven has many firsts. It was the year that I received my first salary and gave it all to Mom (cue: the best daughter award). I realized that I am a tiger treated like a cat in a romantic relationship (another form of abuse, and yes, of course, I'll tell you about my romances, not in this book). I had too much freedom for the first time in my life (playing Ariana Grande songs in the background).

Through all the pains, I realized that the hearsays of moving forward is true. Moving forward starts with acceptance. It is the first step in making a change when change is possible. It is the door to the staircase of finding peace of mind when change is not possible. In my case, God has blessed me so much to be telling the story now. Evolution and God's lead have brought me here. Still broken but healed through the love of Christ, my godsend husband, family, and friends. It is possible.

The breakup with my second relationship was life changing. Our love story would make an excellent book. We met in college before I was Miss Congeniality. He hurt me, but I would never erase the pages of him in my life if given a chance. I, before him, was ruthless and insensitive. If he didn't break into my world, I wouldn't discover how wonderful it is to be outside. Despite his shortcomings, he was the one who taught me how to be thoughtful and prioritize family above all else. Part of why I discovered I love surprises is because he is the first person who throws me one. He has all the tricks to making a girl feel loved and appreciated. Probably, his goal in life is to treat his woman like a princess. Unfortunately, when I grew up, I realized I was not the princess type.

It took me a while to reach acceptance. Because of my childhood pains, I was so idealistic with relationships. My Mom had so many men that I aimed to have one—losing him was like losing a dream to spend the rest of my life with my first love. I exhaust the first eight months of freedom from my first long-term relationship, from September twenty-zero-seven until May twenty-zero-eight, partying and getting wild. I have no regrets but gratitude to God and the world's kindness for keeping me safe through all those "adventures," which is too inappropriate to be part of this book. Maybe soon if I have the inspiration again. I would do a tell-all of what those adventures are. Remembering them is just too much for now.

That first job and heartbreak opened a floodgate of opportunities. When I was in those moments of pain, I wondered if what I know now while looking back at those times would matter. Probably yes, but I wouldn't want it the other way. The things that happened in the past, all the hardships that I experienced as a child and as a young adult, are treasures that made me who I am today. I am now fully aware of my mental health and the coping mechanism that kept me sane.

The four years on the first job saw me managing work on top of the Filipino eldest child's responsibility of being a breadwinner. I have worked for at least four other IT (Information Technology) companies in Cebu, where my first company had a subcontracting engagement. I was happy because even though I only have enough for my family and rely on some essentials on my boyfriend-now-husband, I have managed, or at least I thought I have.

Musing over the events that led me to my second company was a mix of pride and prejudice. Reading back my blog entries of July twenty-eleven made me cringe at my apparent need for attention and shameful tendencies to "padungog-dungog." I knew my blog could be helpful to me someday, but now that I'm reading back on it and realized so many things, I would like to congratulate my twenty-five-year-old self for making it happen.

I initially didn't hear the call to move on and find a new job, despite the onset of Mom's sickness at twenty-eleven. Maybe the busyness has drowned the call. I didn't see it coming. April twenty-eleven had been a stressful month. Whining has been my refuge. My then-three-year-boyfriend-now-husband, tired of my constant rambles, coaxed me into finding a new job. I had countless reasons not to. He answered my litany with, "Ingna lang gyud na loyal ka!" The line gets to me. It somehow hurt as if loyalty was a mistake. By mid-May, I posted my updated resume online. I got calls, but being busy still, I turned down some and rescheduled the others. Some didn't call me back, which oddly makes me happy. Some persevered. However, my heart is just not ready for a new job.

Come June, finally, the busyness reached a die down. I got a call from two companies. I was still hesitant, but being not too busy, I focused. Maybe if something was really for you, then the universe will conspire for its realization. That's what happened to me. I just went there, all prepared with my new blouse bought by the supportive then-three-year-boyfriend-now-husband, expecting the worst, yet went home well but confused. It seems so flowing that I think it's flawed. I thought I couldn't get the job. The hiring manager waived the exam and directly processed me for an interview. He knew me from college. We were in the same scholar group and the supreme student government.

The interview was remarkable. I had fun talking to all my interviewers. Though they assured me to call three days later, I still didn't feel at ease the day after the interview. When the exhilaration dies down, a thought dawn on me. My clothes were all in the laundry so, I chose to wear the clothes from the interview at the office. I never expected the call early. With no time to return to the boarding house, I wore the same blouse from the interview to the job offer at different days. Fast-forward, when I became a regular member of the team at my second company, one of my interviewers at that time commented that he thought that my first company had a uniform. Laugh out loud! When I went back to the office of my first job, I composed my resignation letter to the surprise of my teammates as there was no sign about the resignation at all.

The second job offered a salary higher than my first job. I couldn't realize the positive financial implications of the new position. I didn't see it as an answer to my problem of financing Mom's operation during that time; pondering about it now warms my heart because of how my story at my second company unfolded. Just like my transition from my first to second job, it was God's doing. Both times ended in growth, leading to a new season. Freedom when I transferred into my second company while motherhood, four months into my third company.

> "What you do makes a difference, and you have to decide what kind of difference you want to make."

My first job saw me grow from a sheltered, self-conscious girl into an empowered woman aware of her strength. Unbeknownst to me, my second job was a portal to a new world of self-discovery. The blessings never stop flowing. During my first year, I got a promotion. Considered for a team lead role in my second year, when I didn't get the part, I was sent to a six-month assignment abroad in April of twenty-thirteen. When I returned, I got another promotion to a senior developer. It was also the time that the then-boyfriend-now-husband proposed. We got married in March of twenty-fifteen. After which, we trekked most of the mountains in Cebu and some famous mountains in the Philippines. I was no longer surviving but thriving. My second company has provided me so much love and comforts that I have grown not only at work but personally. Then comes the crisis. Mom had bipolar in July of twenty-seventeen.

On the tenth of July, twenty-seventeen, I received a call that kick off the events leading to my sudden departure. I wasn't looking for a job, but the headhunter was quite persistent, it got me into the grind. However, the job required a skill that has long been buried. Being reminded of it got me excited. Not wanting to tarnish my name by not showing up on the day of the technical interview, despite not being able to review, a little voice in my head nudged me to attend because I needed the skills updated. I thought the interview was a suitable venue for me to relearn my craft. I was unaware that the Lord was cooking something better. By God's grace, I passed the technical interview and was ushered for a final interview. At noon on the same day, I was scheduled for a job offer. I was shocked. I left the hiring office with a heavy heart, very opposite to how most people would feel after getting a job. Confusion, sadness, and a mixture of negative and positive emotions dragged me to unconsciously ride a jeepney to my second company's office — my home for the last six years.

When I sat down on my desk, it was then that the confusion got stronger. What should I do? I messaged friends and asked for advice. I read articles about what to consider when accepting a job offer. I called the agent that got me into the dilemma and shared my hesitations. None of them made me feel better. After some silence, I opened my blog and read posts. It got me away from my confusion. When I read the posts about my mom, I paused. I didn't ask God for anything at that moment of silence. Me before would have asked for signs on what to decide, but I knew better.

As a child of God, we should not follow signs and wonders. Signs and wonders follow us. When I came back to the hiring office, there was no decision yet. But I have listed things for consideration. Things to consider when accepting a job offer: Compensation Package Benefits; Perks; Work Environment; Shift Schedule; Job Description; Work

Culture; Flexibility; Deadline of job offer Decision; When to start; Work-Life Balance. I read the documents from cover to cover, thoroughly scrutinizing every detail. Without knowing yet the salary and the job description, the perks already got me interested. When they laid out the two primary considerations, I was in awe, thinking how God is just the best. It was too much to let go of. The Lord blew me away. It was the job that I've been preparing and training for, since twenty-thirteen, as a Team Lead. The salary increase was an answered prayer, even though I didn't ask for it out loud. God just knows I needed it for the sudden expense due to Mom's illness. I wasn't looking for a job, but it turns out God knows better. He saw through my sufferings. The silent screams of my heart that I was too busy to notice or choose not to notice. I was happy, comfortable, and loved. Why would I want more? Because God thinks I deserve more than what I thought I deserved. When you've been self-sabotaging yourself for years, putting yourself down and believing you are not worthy of more can become the normal. I'm super thankful that God knew what I needed. He led me through and filled in where I lacked.

After I accepted the offer, I was still at odds. To stay or walk away? Was my decision, right? The day after I got the job, God answered. I learned that my Mom tried to escape from the center. The doctor had to lift the no visit policy. We can visit at least once a week. Seeing her was an eye-opener. She surprisingly looks good but is still unwell. For my Mom to function normally, she needs me to support her, both emotionally and financially. And yes, I needed that raise. The day after I was hired, during our Church Sunday service, our pastor's talk was the second eye-opener, especially the fourth point — use the story of your loss to share the story of the cross. I haven't lost anything, but things are changing after I surrendered my life to Jesus. I was brave and strong, but with God, I was more. God was at work in my life way before I was baptized in the spirit. I understood more of His promises of glory to glory when I developed an intimate relationship with Him. There was an understanding that the same God who gives me the suffering will be the same God that will deliver me from it. When my Mom got into the center, I trusted in Him wholeheartedly. Not once did I stop to ask why I deserve to undergo the kind of trial that I'm going through. I chose to see the roses in the thorns.

In between my life's crisis since I started working in twenty-zero-seven to twenty-eleven, there were dark moments that I wanted to stop and end everything. Overwhelmed with the responsibility to pay my Mom for her sacrifices with raising me alone, support my brother to school and attend even to the needs of my Uncle's family, who had raised me when Mom was away at work. I troubled myself with the thought that my Mom raised me to be an investment. Compared to my brother and cousins, I had a different upbringing. They did all the housework as I was often left to study. I am the princess of the house. My want to give back what I have owed them drove me to work harder than I should. I was so consumed with giving them a good life that I forgot that I have my life too. During those moments of suffering, my fear of failure, and the need for control due to my built-in self-sabotage, I had days were the thought of dying is so strong.

CHAPTER FOUR— MANAGING SELF-SABOTAGE

In June of twenty-seventeen, I had the urge to let go of something I love most in my second job — employee ambassadorship. It was an excruciating decision, as I didn't know why God planted the idea in my head. Still shocked with the decision not to be involved in employee engagement anymore, by the start of July, God asked to let go of another thing — the women's organization. The idea to restructure the leadership to give more women an avenue to practice leading was just born in my head, so I could make myself dispensable. I didn't know why I had to let go, but I know I just had to let God. For most of the story of my life, my blind faith in the almighty has taken me places that, if I relied on my capacity, is unreachable.

To wrap up my excellent time being an employee

ambassador, my words of goodbye have hinted at something big. When I reread the post, it amazed me at how things unfold as it would seem in my open letter that I know I am about to resign, which was not the case. What I know is that I just followed God's lead.

> An open letter to all those who have made my Ambassadorship incredible and memorable:

This open letter is not a goodbye but a message of gratitude for all the happy memories I will bring with me as I chase a new dream. I have thought and prayed about this for a while. Even as I am writing, there's still doubt how I will survive giving up something that I love to do. But I trust in God's guidance and wisdom. Ever since I accept Him as my personal Lord and Savior, things are changing inside me. Every day, He helps me focus on the things that matter most. Leaving the ambassadorship is hard. I enjoyed doing what I do despite the challenges that come with it, but I understand that sometimes we need to give up something good for something better. I don't know yet what better things God will have for me, but I am open to anything. In my pursuits of happiness and contentment, I have put God at the bottom of my priority and made those that make me happy bigger than Him. It stops now.

I pray that even if I am gone from this great circle bonded by our mutual love to give happiness to our fellow employees, you will all continue. I will not be gone, you can still ask me for guidance and help, but that's it. The choice to renew and not be super active like I did since becoming an ambassador in twenty-fifteen is there, yet my conscience won't let me. I cannot be part of something without working at it. I must be involved. Some of you may have realized that I have been planning this for now. I'm having second thoughts, but after the recent activities, the fitness challenge, and the summer outing, all of it was gone. You are all so incredible that it assures me that the happiness will continue.

Being a neophyte ambassador in twenty-fifteen was hard. I expected too much. Yet out of those disappointments and hurts, I returned in twenty-sixteen carrying the lessons I learned from the previous year. But after the announcement of the twenty-sixteen ambassadors, knowing that out of the four kindred spirits in twenty-fifteen, I prevailed but the only one left, my fire flickered. But God gave me hope.

I thank God for He led me to extraordinary people. If you are reading this, that's YOU. Thank you so much! All the activities, the meetings, and everything we did together were super spectacular. It makes me cry. Teamwork is one of my soft spots, and every time I think of the teams that we have created warms my heart. Thank you so much. I cannot mention all of you, but you must know that you are all in a special place in my heart. Believe that you are!

I thank God for giving me a partner who is just so awesome. You know who you are. Thank God for you. Continue to lead with kindness and by heart. You are a one-of-a-kind leader. I would always cherish the decisions that we made together. It was always my prayer to find someone like you. Thank you for always lending a helping hand even before you became an ambassador.

Thank God for the fabulous ladies who move heaven and earth to support me despite everything. My husband is the wind beneath my wings, but the trust and support you ladies extended empower me to do great things. I'm sharing with you a little secret. My bravery comes from people like you who believe I can make a difference. Thank you! Let's focus on creating the organization that we dream about. As shared in our meeting, let's shift our focus to quality, not quantity. We don't need many to do great things. Kisses to you all, my lovely ladies. You are the best. Be proud of what we have done so far...and be excited about what we will do.

And the most excellent thanks to God are for admin, shout out to two extraordinary ladies and everyone in management, and the company. Thank you so much for all the support. After almost six years of staying in the company, I still think that being here is God's gift. I am happy to be doing my job and my passion for organizing events and bringing people together.

I used to think that this is not the company for me, as it seemed dull when I was new at twenty-eleven. Oh well, it's not that the company is boring. I was the boring employee. When I stopped being that employee, I realized that there is so much life in where I am. I feel so blessed to have been a part of that life. Now my life is overflowing that I think I need to step back to share the life that I enjoyed.

Again, this letter is not a goodbye as I intend to stay, but I owe it to everyone who makes my ambassadorship exciting to say farewell. I have always been anxious and worrisome about what people will think, even if God has kept reassuring me that I don't need to. This is my way of saying thank you for the chance to serve and a lasting reminder of just how much fun I had been as one of the ambassadors. This letter is also a call to all those who want to be ambassadors to grab the chance to be one.

Today is the thirty-first of July, twenty-twenty-one as of writing. It makes my heart funny as it is the fourth anniversary of the day that I passed my resignation back on the thirty-first of July, twenty-eleven.

There's a heaviness in my heart after I handed in my resignation letter. The idea that I'm leaving is still painful. And as I talked to a friend about it, tears flowed. I'm worried that I might be crying every day until the last day. Hopefully not. There's no easy goodbye, but sometimes, goodbyes are inevitable. It's the natural course of life. We leave, or other people go, creating a strange feeling of loss. I decided to start a personal journey of goodbye where I will write my feelings and the activities that I did to cope up with the monumental decision.

Leaving my first job back in twenty-eleven after working for four years was hard but leaving my second job is more brutal. It has been my home for six years, one month and fourteen days, including my last day on the thirty-first of August, twenty-eleven. I love the company a lot. But sometimes, love is not enough to make you stay. It's painful to say goodbye, but when God asks you to, who are you to say no?

If we focus on the pain, it will cripple us. But if we look beyond, we understand that the pain is the start of something new. We must look past our circumstances to comprehend that what we have been provided, even if it is painful, and we think we are not ready, is what we deserve and in God's plan. In the end, it is not our plans but God's who will prevail. So, we must always cheer up and be bold about the future. Trust in His plans. Take a step forward, even if we don't see where the whole staircase will lead. Hold on to Romans eight-

twenty-eight.

> And we know that in all things, God works for the good of those who love him, who have been called according to his purpose. — Romans 8:28 (NIV)

Despite the discomfort and the pain of leaving my second company, which has become my comfort zone for six years, I pushed through. I didn't understand in June why God had asked me to let go of things. When July rolled in, as narrated in the previous chapter, I was called into a job that I didn't apply for and was eventually hired to my third company. From the pain of letting go of something I loved to more when my Mom had bipolar disorder, God turned it into a purpose by calling me into my new company.

Despite the gains of leaving, the pain was inevitable. My second job saw my professional and personal growth. It is the start of everything from traveling to trekking to organizing events to owning a condo to the first out-of-the-country experience to starting a rental business to marriage. Being in the company has cemented my confidence in influencing others. I was brave, but I'm bolder under its wing. It has provided me with many avenues to be so much more than I was. It's hard to leave. But why did I still choose to go? Because I had to. It's too early to settle. Being in the company has provided me with so much that it made me less ambitious. The comfort zone blinded me with the opportunities provided. The strong ties with the people kept me from asking for more. Being wired differently, I realized that staying after a chance for growth knocks is scarier than leaving to start from zero at a new company.

Did I plan to leave? No. I am a woman with a plan but starting a new life in September of twenty-seventeen is never a part of it. But as I was looking back at the events leading to the resignation, I realized how exceptional God is. Without me knowing it, leaving must have been God's grand plan all along. As a new Christian in June of twenty-seventeen, I prayed more than I ever was. As a woman of control, transitioning to Christian life where you put God first in everything was hard.

Let GO. Let GOD! With all the uncertainty, the fear of starting again, and leaving my comfortable life behind, my only option is to trust in Him, who has been blessing me with so much. Every day I woke up grateful for all that He had done in my life, even before I had this intimate relationship with Him. When asked how I'll move on? God is the answer.

As cheesy as it sounds, I believe God pulls me out of my second company for a purpose. I have seen how focused on building myself to be used by God more. Regardless of what people say, the only impression that would matter is God's. People can think of anything, but I will stand firm in His promises.

The Good In Goodbye

As soon as the alarm sounded on my last day at work, I tried to keep the morale high. I knew I needed more to go through the day. Despite the flesh call to check on Facebook first to wake me up, I opened my bible to read my devotional. My devotional was titled "Just Love." It talked about how even the lowest of sinners is forgiven. God is a God of forgiveness. No matter how much we sinned, He will always forgive us if we repent and accept that we are sinners.

As I related above to my last day of work in my second company, I realized that of my six years, I never really had significant issues with anyone. Still, I'd be lying if I said there wasn't an instance where I was tempted to unleash my fury and act with pride.

The temptation to act rashly, out of vain conceit and pride, was an everyday struggle. But throughout every opportunity, I am thankful that I have remained humble and thought of others first before myself. I have never let influence and power get into my head. I stayed faithful in my values of giving happiness, expecting nothing in return. Seeing others happy and enjoying my efforts was enough. All of it boils down to just love. It's the love of people, the love of fun, and the love of God.

When I resigned from my first job, the goodbyes lasted for a week. I scheduled coffee dates, karaoke sessions, and other meet-ups. I even wrote a whole memoir of the people who have touched my life, plus a look back at how I spent my four years in the company. Although I didn't get the chance to do it when I left my second company, I created a photo book instead. It was hard to narrate everything because I didn't know where to start and fit everything in a single post. There were so many people and events that it overwhelmed me. But I know if I don't write or make something out of my memories, I will keep looking back and won't start fresh from my new workplace.

So, how was my last day? It wasn't as tearful as I thought it would be. When I walked out the door, I sent flying kisses to those who stood and clapped. I was sad to go, but there was peace in my heart. God kept on reassuring me that leaving was His plan. I don't have to worry about anything because He will always be with me.

The goodbye was simple but full of love. From the two-thousand gift certificate received from the company recognition platform, I bought eight dozen Krispy Kreme donuts. I distributed it to my team, ladies, and other friends. Because it was also the Filipiniana General Assembly for the ladies, I brought some puto (sticky rice) too.

At my last team meeting, I took photos of my team

and selfies. They pressured me into saying a goodbye speech. The speech was impromptu, but I was glad to say my goodbye.

Goodbye with the ladies then followed the team meeting. I expected something from them, but they somehow exceeded my expectations. While I enjoyed their actions, I felt happier and more ready to go. Power women sang a song. Sisterhood made a tribute video. Wonder Women made a scrapbook. And as an exit wave, I made my last speech.

In the middle of eating the food prepared, some of my ambassador and trekking friends arrived. It was only then that I realized that it's almost time to go. After a long chat, the three helped me clean up and brought my things back to my desk. It was time to go. By six, I left the office escorted by a friend, who I just learned last week was also in my third company now. He walked with me to the husband's office. For a while, it confused me why I didn't shed a tear when I left. As I pondered, it was maybe because I had shed enough tears when I shared the news of my resignation. They were sad but fully supported my growth and this new chapter of my life. I already shed tears for the memories, so when I left, there was nothing left to cry for. Working in my second company has been a journey of everything for me. My first company saw the worst version of me. In my second company, I had spread my wings and have learned to manage self-sabotage. Now, at my third company,

I prayed for maturity. Foreshadowed a time that I get out of my me-circle and explore. God answered my prayers and more.

CHAPTER FIVE-HERE COMES MOTHERHOOD

On the twenty-second day of September twenty-seventeen, I started my first day at my third job. I was a newbie, fresh blood, new joiner. Having worked in the industry for ten years, I remember little of the first day as a newbie in my first or second job. I wish I had written how it felt back then, but maybe like how I procrastinated writing what I felt, it must have been the same case.

The thought of writing has been on my mind after the new job orientation. I had fun learning about my new home. There were lots of surprises as I didn't take the time to research it when I attended the job interview (I should have). And as I learned more about my third company, it made me realize how being here is indeed God's best.

The opportunity for learning and growth is unlimited. The services provided to clients with end-to-end solutions also open endless possibilities for talents to learn a new craft while working in expertise. I have always wanted to learn more about human resources and recruitment. It's too early to tell yet, but I'm happy to know that the avenue is available.

Work-life balance is still within reach. When I shared that I'd be transferring here, people scared me off, saying I would lose my freedom and the perks of a work-life balance. Of course, I was ready for the change, but there were hesitations and disbelief. Facilitators last Friday and some friends assured me that work-life balance is still within reach. Everything is still up to you. They have splendid avenues for communities.

The new company makes me feel like a part of something big with a heart for those I value the most. With its global reach and having one global network as part of its six core values, it gives me endless opportunities to connect with like-minded individuals all over the world. I also love how it emphasizes respect for individuals, especially LGBT, and providing health coverage to life partners (unmarried partners).

I have many hopes and dreams brought by knowing my new home more, plus the expectations and challenges of my new job role. The best thing about getting a new job for me is the opportunity to change something about myself without raising eyebrows or suspicions of mental illness. I have wanted to withdraw from the spotlight and people for a while now, but because I want to avoid creating a stir for changing from Miss Congeniality, I struggled.

I remembered how during orientation, instead of talking to my fellow new joiners while waiting, I read my bible devotional. When it started, I waited and observed, very different from the usual me. Thankfully, even with my change, I had connected and knew outstanding people.

Getting the job was a journey of faith. From the hiring process to the actual job start was a test of how strong my faith was in God. And even as I continued my journey in the company.

Whether it is pure luck or the law of attraction working on the shadows of my deployment notice on the eighteenth of October twenty-eleven, I only hold on to one thing— obedience to God. Since the beginning of the new chapter of my life, God has been my pillar. Worldly woes tempted me, urging me to focus only on myself to secure stability, but in the end, God would always remind me of His promise.

> I pulled you out of your comfort zone for a reason, Kring. It is not your will but mine. My plans for you are in progress. Do not worry nor be impatient about anything. Just obey and continue to let your light shine so that others will know Me through you.

Trusted God despite the worries of a delayed starting or hire date. I left my previous company on the thirty-first of August. The eighth of September was my start date. The background check took a while, so they moved it to the fifteenth of September and finally to the twenty-second of September. The day of waiting from the postponed date to the still unsure hire date was a battle of faith and worldly fears. "What ifs" crept into my head, and the separation anxiety took a toll. Self-sabotage got me in a cycle of mental crisis because I had no one to share the uneasiness of uncertainty. The enemy then took the opportunity to make me question the things I do for people.

> Too many friends, but no one reaches out in your time of need. It's all over your blog, but like always, no one takes the hint. Stop reaching out to people because, for all you know, they don't care. People remember you when they are sad or needing something; otherwise, you're just an acquaintance. Do you have friends?

It was a bloody battle within. I succumbed, but only for a time; I realized it was wrong to rely on friends when I have a big God behind me. I shift focus to enjoy my downtime and thanked God for the extended vacation. It turns out I needed it. The church services have helped as well. Tuesday's prayers opened opportunities to deepen my prayer life, and it gave me the confidence to pray aloud. Bible study Thursday enabled me to strengthen my faith in His word.

The first postponement no longer bothered me. Even the fact that for the first time, I won't have a salary for three pay periods. Often, when things go well, our trust in God is sure. Yet, when things happen, we forget about God's plan for our life.

When I continue to pursue His word by attending services and focusing on the positive of the postponements, I showed God my obedience. The silver linings of vacation, and provisions for my monthly payments, were assurances that God is in control. Instead of panic, I renewed and deepened my faith in His plan. I stopped relying on friends to keep me sane. The joy of my first day felt excellent, knowing it was a fruit of my obedience and reliance on God.

It is hard to continue being faithful to God when we are confused with what is happening, but if we focus on His promise of a good life for all His children, we should be okay. Let us always remember that trials are only there to sharpen and strengthen us. Always see the gain out of the pain. Stay positive and remain in obedience to His will. It will amaze you how He can twist the tides in our favor. When God promises something, He is always faithful to His promise, but that doesn't mean that everything would be easy.

After overcoming the momentary setback of the delayed hire date, I thought that was it. It turns out God is not done with His sharpening on me yet by sending me off to the talent pool instead of getting deployed to a project immediately. Being in the talent pool after the excitement of a new job and hearing negative feedback about the place once again tested my faith in Him.

Frustrated by my new predicament and the tons of mandatory training, instead of letting my light shine, the grind dulled me. But I felt uneasy with the negative aura: bored or scared or wrapped up in the wrong beliefs being in the talent pool. I know I needed to do something, but I waited for God to seize the opportunity. While waiting, I equipped myself and remained positive, even if surrounded by negativity. Overcoming the last hurdle taught me to trust in God more and never worry about anything. It is by God's grace that I am here, and I assured myself that He doesn't do things without reason.

In between the mandatory training, I gained and collected knowledge of my new company by connecting to friends already in the company and reading many available resources. Frustration turned to gratitude when I realized the opportunity to know my company at a high level, which is impossible had I been deployed to a project immediately. Being in the talent pool is a blessing.

By the second week at work, I wanted to finish the training first before sharing my light was the plan.

But God has other things in mind. Despite being reminded by my new friends to focus on the mandatory instead of helping, I listened to God's voice. I cannot contain my desire to spread God's light to motivate the other trainees, which were mainly younger than me.

To be with persons who don't share the same passion towards people was my resistance. Someone teased me about being a politician for wanting to help. They had this "what's in it for me?" heartbreaking attitude, but instead of being discouraged, I obeyed God's command to be Jesus's ambassador wherever I go.

By the end of the second week, God compelled me to release my gift of writing, talking, and organizing. I asked them how they felt about being in the talent pool. With the responses, I learned a lot about the culture. Thanks to God, they trusted me. I used my organizing skills on our first Friendly Friday activity. The activity was successful, even if I planned it on the fly–another evidence of God's work.

By the third week, trainees would have been death bored, they say. Imagine the pressure when I realized I'm not even halfway through my mandatory training. I wondered what I had done wrong for not being death bored yet. I spent the first day of that week checking on my list of to-dos. Because of a two-day training, I need to ensure I miss nothing.

The training was a blast and an eye-opener. By talking to other participants (long-time employees) about my status, they opened their experiences as well as assuring me that "I am not alone."

The third week ended on a high note from the training and the second friendly Friday on a salary day when I brought puto in celebration. To encourage new friends to join our church concert, I gave out five tickets to the winners.

Week four kicked off with excellent training. The first training was an eye-opener, but the second training was inspirational. I was more fired up to do more at the talent pool. I met many incredible people who were very supportive to the point of making my problem our team's problem during the design thinking training:

> How might we help Kring promote proper awareness by removing the demotivating mindset and encouraging self-skill-up?

The action made me realize God would send people to help you. He is always there like He promises. Aside from my design thinking team, the facilitator was an inspiration, too.

When I went back to the talent pool after another fantastic time with God at Tuesday prayer, I was even more inspired to share what I have learned with the junior trainees. I wasted no time and asked the facilitator to organize a Witty Wednesday to share what I learned from my two training sessions. Early in the morning, before I facilitated the activity, I received a deployment notice. God finally answered my prayers. I was so amazed at God's timing. It's as if He purposely scheduled the activity for me to be able to share before I leave.

Since attending the first training, I already have a department in mind. From talking to one of the attendees, he gave me an idea of a department. When I returned to the training office, I shared with my new seatmate about my preferred department. And because God is exceptional, they indeed deployed me to the department that I wanted to be, prompting her to say that the law of attraction was so strong in me. I replied that it's not about the law of attraction but God's will.

In the talent pool, there are three suggested activities to break the monotony of online training: Motivation Monday, Witty Wednesday, and Friendly Friday. The trainees shall organize, but no one took the initiative. I did. Aside from sharing what I learned from the training, I also encouraged them to join the movement. To continue the fun in learning, even if I leave, I grouped the remaining trainees into three to practice scrum. Each team owns a center activity where they can use design thinking to host a Motivation Monday, Witty Wednesday, or Friendly Friday.

Before leaving, I met with each team to discuss

their goals and said goodbye. I was sad to leave as I feel I haven't done enough yet, but after talking to them, I realized it was more than enough. God did a good job. I was happy to be an instrument of His love to these young people who badly need a burst of inspiration.

Getting into the talent pool was my promised land after days of waiting for my start date. I encountered opposition and resistance in fulfilling my purpose, but in the end, God has helped me put things together. And as a product of my obedience, they deployed me at last. I was thrilled to realize that I didn't leave the talent pool the way I have found it. It is tempting to focus on our problem, but throughout the stories of my life, I have learned that my circumstances don't matter to my capacity to help. For my problems, I have God, so I'm free to help others with their problems.

It is human to focus on our good and think of ourselves first before others. But being Jesus's ambassador, He called us to deny our human nature and strive to be Jesus everywhere we go. It is a hard path, but God values obedience to His will. Part of obedience is showing God's kindness without expecting anything in return. One thing that keeps us from getting to where God wants us to be is our disobedience. Our misery is not a hindrance to help others get out of their misery. If God called you to help, even in challenging circumstances, and you obey unquestionably, God will surely get you out of it. God promised glory to all those who follow His word. Keep on obeying God and see how He transforms your life around.

CHAPTER SIX — THE WANDERFULL LIFE

As we move into the next part, let's do a recap. What have you learned so far? Think for a minute, then continue. I hope you find value in what you are reading, even if this book is for me to assess my feelings that my life is not that bad compared to what I perceive. That despite the self-sabotage, mental struggles of an extroverted new mom in denial of a need for authentic human connection in the pandemic, it is in my prayer that this can help you, too. A mid-thirty crisis at the time of Covid-19 is unprecedented. A mental turmoil is difficult, but it is especially challenging this time. Before we resume our walk, you can pause and visit the blog created to help connect with you who may want to join, where you can post a comment or share about your feels upon reading my book: https://WNFRat35.wordpress.com/

The weight of the mid-thirty crisis is no joke. While I am aware of yearly mental meltdowns or pre-birthday blues as every year when my birth month starts, I just have this obsession or compulsion to do something different. Marking the new age is the goal, and feeling the blues now is extra heavy. It feels like every day is Monday. For a person who is very much aware of her mental strength through faith, it is confusing how the crisis never left despite the intimacy with God. The cycle of depression and mania is mentally and emotionally exhausting. Nothing feels right, and everybody seems out to get me. This episode is alarming because it started months before my birth month. Signs began in January. In the last week of January twenty-twenty, I created a video detailing my work burnout to share my feelings with my Life Group. It has been a while since I attended our sessions. Because I have promised them an update, I prepared my sharing beforehand. I never thought that burnout would turn into a mental crisis.

February and March were quite busy with weekend activities to escape the stress at work. The unusual mental exhaustion peaked. All I wanted to do was give everything up. I questioned many things and have gone extra doubtful. When an opportunity at work opened to answer some doubts, I took it. But instead of helping, the growing crisis has developed into a full-blown disaster. I know

I needed professional help, but I was stubborn to accept that perhaps God put the idea in my head to seek help. I didn't ask for help. Looking back at what happened through the eyes of someone who just survived a storm, I know I should have. However, I'm eternally grateful to God that even though I didn't obey in seeking professional help, He didn't leave. My husband has been my guiding post through the storm. Three months of pain from April to June were mental. Crazy thoughts manifested into physical pains for me and the entire household. By the third week of June, on our thirteenth anniversary as boyfriend and girlfriend, the husband had bad diarrhea that canceled our plans. I was eagerly awaiting our trip to escape the complicated feelings. The tiny thread that holds my mental state snapped. Despite his condition, I went into a mental breakdown.

It was probably our most extended fight, with me screaming at every chance I got. I threw all the wrong words and things that made me feel ill at him. He didn't deserve my wrath, but I am forever grateful to this man who stood by me, warts and all. Remembering and writing the exact moments is very painful, not because of what I feel but what I did to my husband. He never likes it when I tell people he is the superman behind wonder woman, but truthfully, he is. I cannot imagine my life if God didn't ask me to wait for him during our first date. You might think that the story of how my husband is the savior of my twenty-twenty-one crisis is unrelated to this chapter's topic of fun. However, when I had my first significant crisis, the mid-twenty crises, the then-boyfriend-now-husband was the same person who introduced FUN to my life to divert my mind from the situation. Before twenty-eleven, blogging and scrapbooking were the only fun that I knew. The trip, treks, and board gaming were unheard of.

As a frustrated writer or novelist, I write all sorts of things. I love to learn and decided to explore how to write in a sort-of-reporter-kind-of-way at a blog that I created at work in my first year of being an employee Ambassador back in twenty-fifteen. I write or blog to remember the exciting things that I've experienced. But it makes me happy to know that people got inspired by the things that I write. The husband and I started trekking and board gaming as a couple in twenty-eleven after three years of being in a roller-coaster relationship and the onset of my mid-twenty crisis. I can be very jealous and volatile when it comes to love life. But the then-boyfriend-now-husband made me better and supported me to reach the best version of myself through our wander-filled life. Fun for me are my birthday celebrations over the years and the significant milestones from twenty-five to thirty. I don't remember much about my birthdays before twenty because I don't have pictures to remind me of them. Looking back at the birthday photos in my archive, I was amazed to realize that I always have different celebrations and hairs each year. I didn't do it on purpose. Celebrating it with other people is not a plan too.

Curly hair at twenty-two. Straight hair at twenty-three. Straightened hair at twenty-four. Boy hair at twenty-five. Short hair at twenty-six. So, on. Changing my hair or traveling are my go-to celebrations. Too bad, both are not possible in this quarantine. I think I will remember my thirty-fifth birthday differently through this book. Birthday flashbacks of my twenty-second birthday to twenty-four saw me spending each year with different groups. I spent my twenty-second birthday at a popular barbecue location in my place of work with six other couples. Out of the six, only one other couple aside from us ended up in marriage. The rest didn't survive. It will be awkward to celebrate with them again. For my twenty-third birthday, I had an overnight stay at my favorite beach with the singles crowd: my brother's friends and my best friends. On my twenty-fourth birthday, I had a multi-celebration from the office to the mall, wrapped up in a karaoke session. Now that I am collating these events of my life, I realized just how awesome God is for putting things together. The multi-celebration of my twenty-fourth birthday feels like closure to an era.

The following years were me embracing the remarkable change I encountered year after year.

Twenty-five was my defining year, celebrated on a trip that I paid for on my own for the first time with two of my girlfriends. Twenty-sixth is on a trip to Baguio with work friends. Twenty-seven was spent abroad on a six-month company-sponsored trip in the United States. At twenty-eight, the then-boyfriend-now-husband and I got engaged; as we were saving, we chilled. My twenty-ninth birthday was at dinner with my fabulous family. Spending the last two birthdays before thirty, not on travel, didn't matter, as I feel that my twenty-seventh birthday abroad was a bonus. Besides, the plan was to celebrate my thirties on an international trip. God gave it to me at twenty-seven.

I am just grateful for everything in my life. I thank the Lord for always providing for me, even for the things that I didn't ask. When I turned thirty, I remembered I challenged the thirties to bring it on. I was just so excited to grow up, freeing myself from the burden of the twenties. During the mid-twenty crisis and utterly envious of peers getting engaged and having a baby, I created a dream — thirty-thirty-dot-five. It was a dream to travel to thirty places in Cebu (my hometown), thirty provinces in the Philippines (my home country), and five countries. It was too ambitious for someone who barely had enough to buy a decent cell phone. But I was so down; I needed something to keep me going. I didn't know how to achieve it; I just knew

I wanted it. From my countless blogs, full of complaints and insecurity, before twenty-five, I created another one. This time, it was for the thirty-thirty-dot-five project. I started revisiting my pictures and realized that I was not super pathetic after all compared to what I thought. When I started, I was down to twenty-twenty-seven-dot-five. I have already been to ten places in Cebu from company outings and gatherings. Three locations in the Philippines for the boyfriend-paid trips since twenty-o-eight. Boyfriend's goal is a trip outside of Cebu. And of course, no countries as I only got my passport because it's a requirement of my second job which landed on my lap only in July of twenty-eleven.

Around May twenty-eleven, I read about a peso sale for a local airline without really doing anything about my dream. Without second thoughts, I booked and did not consider raising the money to spend on the trip. The only thing that's clear to me is that I had to support myself. The trip was a blast. I was able to achieve my first triumph in wanders. It was my first organized and paid trip since I started working at twenty-o-seven. On April twenty-thirteen, I was chosen as one of the ten employees to travel to our company headquarters in Duluth, Georgia, United States. It was another God's gift. From then on, God's graces and blessings continued to pour in. By March of twenty-sixteen, the husband and I had our first international trip to Hong Kong and Macau to celebrate our first wedding anniversary.

Through all the fun, I would always go back to that fateful day in twenty-eleven that started everything. It was a wake-up call to begin seeing my life as a gift and appreciate the things I have. Instead of looking at the other side of the fence, I started to nurture what's in mine. As a child, I was always envious because I had nothing. But as I grow up, I realized that I'm beautiful and intelligent. It killed envy. However, envy resurrected when the mid-twenty crisis kicked in. I realized that most of my friends are either getting hitched or having a baby while I struggled to provide for my family. If not for my husband, who helped me stir my direction, I don't know what would become of me. I started to see things differently and stop looking at what others have. I realized that there's just so much to live. That not going with the flow can also become a source of happiness. I'm grateful to my then-boyfriend-now-husband, who supported me through the transition.

To welcome my thirtieth birthday, the then-boyfriend-now-husband and I went on our longest adventure backpacking through four countries in Indochina. The preparation kept me from a welcome-thirty crisis. Although the trip was in August after our Hongkong-Macau trip, I started planning by December. I have prepared six itinerary options, but even those weren't enough because we settle with a seventh. There were so many things that I wanted to do. Good thing I had a reality checker. The plan was to start in Siem Reap, Cambodia, to visit the infamous Wats. We don't mind that it's super popular, just as long as we see it up close. Then leave on an overnight bus to do a city tour in Phnom Penh, Cambodia. Our fourth night would be in Saigon or Ho Chi Minh City, Vietnam. From Saigon, that's where most of our issues lie. Going to Hanoi from Saigon via train, then Hanoi to Luang Prabang would cost us thirty-six hours for each leg.

We opted to go back to Phnom Penh, arrive early at night, find a place to crash, then ride the early bus to Vientiane. Do an overnight stay in Vientiane and then Vang Vieng — the land of my dreams!!! It was Brightside's fault why I wanted to go. Brightside is a popular website. A weekend in Vang Vieng is a page in my dream book. After Vang Vieng, we will ride the bus again to Udonthani, Thailand. Why Udon? Because it has direct access to Vang Vieng, we want to avoid going back to Vientiane. Since we will be stopping by Udon, we might as well spend a night there. The last stop is Bangkok and the longest too. We need to recuperate before going back home.

"Expectation versus reality" happened to me in a good way during that trip. Our trip was inspiring enough to kill the fear of having my writings validated by a broader audience. I was inspired to submit two posts to Tripzilla, and as of this writing, the two posts are still alive. The Facebook post had around six thousand likes and nine hundred shares in twenty-sixteen. I still occasionally get inquiries and private messages from strangers asking me for tips and tricks. Each stranger is a reminder of a fun-filled life. Sharing the trip on Tripzilla was good because I learned a lot from the people's comments. While I find our trip within our budget, I realized that it might have been too much for others.

The budget was one hundred thousand pesos, excluding the flight fare and accommodation (prepaid). We spent eighty thousand pesos for four countries, which makes it twenty-thousand pesos per country (ten-thousand pesos per person per country). We found our trip just enough, but for those who find it steep on the budget, I also created a list of tips and tricks to significantly reduce the total backpacking cost. Tripzilla also posted the article and had significant shares. One of our most significant expenses of the trip was the accommodation. While I am adventurous, the husband wanted a sure place to stay. He couldn't imagine us jumping from place to place without proper compromise at hand. We have them all pre-booked in Airbnb around two to three months before the date.

Moreover, we have a listing on Airbnb. We are using it as our primary platform for accommodation is paying it forward. Jumping from one country to the other is expensive. We've spent around fourteen thousand pesos on all land trips since I wanted to experience the border crossings. Call it crazy, but Indochina wouldn't be the same had we flown all over. Expensive and battering, but worth it. We were able to experience traveling in different modes of transport, plus we had a chance to immerse ourselves with the locals. But if allowed to go back, I'd remove Laos from the itinerary. It was crazy going there from Vietnam. Most of the itineraries I saw on the net exclude Laos. I should have listened, but I wanted to experience it for myself. There was also a miscalculation on the flight. It would have been nice to start from Ho Chi Minh City, Vietnam, to Cambodia, to Bangkok, and then end in Laos. But we weren't thinking of the itinerary when we booked. I only allocated around eight thousand pesos for food when I made the plan, but it ballooned to almost twice. Instead of just eating in the streets, we splurged a little. We ate at cafés and enjoyed food to our hearts' desires. I'm a fan of thrift eating too, but we've saved enough to eat nicely, so why shouldn't we? I'm a do-it-yourself girl, but when you only have a day to spend in a city, you can't help but splurge on the easy way. Besides, we only have eleven days of travel in between countries. We need to make use of our time wisely.

The forty thousand pesos is not all spent on an

Indochina trip only. We spent around fifteen thousand pesos on our Manila layover. We also splurged a little on buying stuff like a couple-shirt and souvenirs, which were not part of our plan. I planned the trip for almost eight months since we booked the ticket on the thirty-first of December twenty-fifteen. It was the best eight months of my life. I planned for our Indochina trip longer than I did with our Church wedding. The joy of wandering is remarkable. Much more to me because I loved everything about the trip since the planning. And being able to achieve everything that we planned is mind-blowing. I attributed it all to God, to the good people of the place we've been to, especially to the husband who has been very supportive of everything. Once again, the Lord has shown me that nothing is impossible if you only put your mind and heart into it. People thought it was crazy — four countries in less than two weeks? Who'd do that? We JUST did.

I had a very detailed itinerary on our planning board, but the Indochina trip taught me to be flexible. Putting in the day's goals is way better than obsessively plotting everything. Flexibility is more fun. I loved it when the husband would ask our target place to visit every time we arrived at a new location. Then he will search it on the map and find a way to get us there, either by walking or riding a bus and train. Thank God for a very reliable and direction-savvy husband and travel partner. If it's just me, I wonder what would happen with my zero direction and map reading skills.

From our trip, I realized that no matter what other people tell you, doing what you love is the best thing in the world EVER! We should always go and seize it. WE ONLY LIVE ONCE, so we must make the most out of it. We can't bring possessions to the grave, but memories live forever. When I dreamed for thirty-thirty-dot-five in twenty-eleven, it was just a spur-of-the-moment plan to take my depression away during my mid-twenty crisis. I was super amazed that I had overachieved the local and international trips by turning thirty. Visiting thirty places in my hometown Cebu, thirty provinces in my home country, the Philippines, and five countries might seem like a small achievement at thirty, but when I made that dream, it was BIG and unreachable. God is remarkable. It's just spectacular how I had transformed when I stopped feeling like a victim of fate. When I start to embrace and be content with what I have, everything falls into place. Everything indeed happens for a reason. All the bad things in my life have become a testimony.

If you are reading this and feeling like there's no hope for a better future, trust me, there is. Just keep holding on and try to see the good in the bad. The lessons from my adventures and the growth they brought me along the way will always be proof of a fulfilled life. Before the thirties, I am easily excited, but after wrapping my twenties on a trip to Indochina, I feel more relaxed and just thankful for the wander-less weekends of the thirties. All I want to do is rest, binge-watch television series, and have endless laughter and conversations with friends. But this time, the discussions were no longer about me. I feel so blessed that I wanted to share and make others feel the same.

Appreciating downtimes has become a thing. Being busy was everything before. Now, I make it a point to just say "Yes" to the things that matter. Lie-low-ed on Facebook too. Finally!!! I couldn't imagine a time that Facebook would be an option. Being the social butterfly that I was. Now I only checked it for notifications and messages. I still take pictures, but I rarely post them anymore. I over-Facebook-to update my friends on what's going on, but I realized it was more about me. And I think I have enough. I started favoring the value of good influences over shallow fun as well. My heart overflowed with a new drive — to do things with a renewed purpose. Before, the idea of not spending the weekends on a trek, trip, or playing for fun was so absurd and tedious. Now it was rejuvenating. God blessed me with time to spend with a family in quarantine.

When the quarantine started in March of twenty-twenty, I was one of the few who adjusted quickly, as before that; I was already working from home. There was a time that I got bored because I miss the human connection and the fun outside. I was sad because the pandemic happened when I thought my baby girl was now ready to explore. However, while writing this chapter, I realized that I didn't miss anything. I had my fill of fun. Everything in my life has been timed and executed beautifully. These feelings of an unfulfilled life will pass, too. While I don't appreciate the feelings of this mental crisis, I am happy that I am doing something that makes me happy. Extra nostalgia is a sign of a mid-thirty problem but look where it got me. Here I am, on the sixth chapter of the book from my childhood dream. I am showing how mental I can be in this mental crisis if I mentally and spiritually fight for it! I am praying that you will do something good for yourself too.

CHAPTER SEVEN– HOOKED ON A FITNESS

Eleanor Roosevelt once quoted, "No one can make you feel inferior without your consent." I wish I knew of this quote earlier in life. For as long as I can remember, there was never a point where I was satisfied with my body. I always feel fat and unattractive. I usually cover my insecurities by the clothes I wear and being vain. Comparisons were my thing.

One of the reasons why I was addicted to Facebook is because of the memories. It always awed me how I look so pretty on the throwback each time. The happiness was fleeting, as remorse would often follow. I would then wish to go back in time and tell the teenage version to chill and appreciate who you are. We are a product of our thoughts more than we think we are. Despite our differences in how we grow up, our social status, and all those factors that make us human, one thing we have in common — it's our brain, not our body. I wish to tell the young me of how as time passed, the things that she feels would not matter. All she has to do is hold on and listen to the inner voice that says she is beautiful and loved.

Unfortunately, I never had the chance to travel through time. Thankfully, despite that, the young me seems to have found that she is what she thinks she is. She thinks of happy thoughts. She doesn't let negativity put out her fire. Not only that, but she is more significant than her emotions. She can be anyone that she wants. She never listens to other people telling her she can't. All the power she needs is within her. She doesn't hold back. She can pull off anything if she believes.

Beautiful and unique, she is on fire until she opens her world. If only she knew that an outside force could change everything, causing brokenness, insecurity, and insensitivity. Had she known, attention, acceptance, validation, admiration would surely not be a thing. But she didn't, so here I am, putting back the pieces of what's left.

Personalities and why people do what they do always enamored me. In my mind is a deep desire to know people beyond their facade. I have this longing to learn more about how a person develops a particular character over time instead of physical appearances. I am especially drawn to the broken, to the outcasts, to the misfits, and to those who feel inferior. All I want to do is free them from the chains that were once mine when the young me made a mistake. I want to lend them my strength. I tried to teach them how I get the freedom that I enjoyed when I realized how twisted I had been for letting other people drive my life. However, it was a purpose bigger than I could have imagined.

I realized that because I am too focused on the inside that I may have missed caring for my outside until twenty-ten happened. Talking about fitness is the hardest thing to talk about, as it is the very thing that almost robbed me of the chance to experience one of my life's most enormous fulfillments — motherhood.

In twenty-eighteen, two months before regularization, we received a miracle. I was pregnant despite the apparent signs of incapability. We decided not to share until beyond the dreaded first trimester. But as the days passed since knowing the good news, it felt selfish to keep the miracle to ourselves. Considering how unstable pregnancies are, if we delay sharing, we might never have the chance if something changes in God's plans.

Back in twenty-ten, I was diagnosed with PCOS (Polycystic Ovarian Syndrome) after finally deciding to have my almost seven months of missing menstruation checked. It didn't raise any issue until people noticed that I'd grown fat. Absent menstruation was not a problem because it meant no painful cramps but getting bigger was because I was vain.

After getting scolded for delaying, the obstetrician told me that I might have to take pills for the hormones for life. PCOS (Polycystic Ovarian Syndrome), she says, had no cure, and the dangers of infertility are great. I didn't mind infertility, as, at that time, having a baby was the last thing on my mind. What scared me more was the thought of weight gain, hair growth, and acne. She took meds to forced menstruate and gave me a prescription for pills. That started my love-hate relationship with drugs over the years. And the obsession with anything fitness.

For a somewhat demure twenty-four-year-old me, sharing that I was taking pills was a bit shameful. My first memory of drugs was seeing my mom take them because she wants to avoid getting pregnant, considering her scandalous affairs. As I grew, I thought taking medications was shameful. But there I was, to keep my hormones at bay, I needed to take it. For the first few months, I kept the PCOS struggle alone until I got ticked off because everyone was always commenting on my weight gain as if saying I am an irresponsible human being. Good Lord if they only knew that I almost ate nothing.

Years passed, PCOS has become a routine, and so do the pills. I was never faithful through and through. I will take them only if I notice that my acne has gone worse or my waist increases in size. Then I started the endless pursuits of exercise fad, from Zumba to Yoga to Muay Thai and many more. Even the trekking was initially PCOS powered.

I was around forty-five kilos upon diagnosis. Obesity was a natural PCOS future, but thanks to my vanity, I managed to toy around normal to overweight. From routine, PCOS has now become an obsession. At twenty-five, the pressures from PCOS, Facebook addiction, and knowing most of my age got hitched or pregnant, I had my mid-twenty crises. Poor me was battling PCOS and still tied to the Filipino Family, The Eldest Responsibility. I felt so helpless and a victim of fate. To cope, I wanted to marry too and have a BABY as in B.A.B.Y but wait. It was then that the weight of PCOS again crushed me. Not only did it destroy my ala Maria Mercedez sexiness (ahem!), it appears that it can also become a significant roadblock to my fertility.

Since PCOS came, the bouts of mood swings and depressions have become a routine. When I learned that hormones could affect your mood, I made it a point to be mindful of my thoughts. I decided that I won't let PCOS win with my moods, but upon reading fertility and PCOS, I gave up. It was something that I'm not prepared to do. Putting my energy into having a baby was too much, so I decided to change my mindset instead. Who needs a baby anyway?

Instead of crying and exhausting energy on my envy (weddings & babies), the then-boyfriend-now-husband introduced me to wander and wonders. As my batchmates counted their motherhood highs, we got busy with our wanderings. We traveled, trekked, and played board games. The desire for motherhood has been entirely off the table. When asked about the desire for motherhood, I would lament how PCOS made it almost impossible, so I decided not to want it instead.

And because we have abundant friends who love us and want to see the mini-us, it has been such a struggle to forget the baby issue completely. There was a time that attending reunions and gatherings became unbearable as a friend's question, and I had to relive the pain all over again so that they would stop tormenting me about pregnancy.

Then I met Jesus in twenty-sixteen. I know God loves me and considers me His favorite. Because if there wasn't any, how else did I manage to evade my dark background of drugs and prostitution? I was loved and protected. No matter the circumstances, God favors me. I thought I had enough of God, and how wrong and proud was I to have thought of such.

Twenty-sixteen was the year of change. It opened me up to a relationship with God that I never thought possible. It was the year that I learned how different religion is to relationships. Religion is about the practice; the relationship is about your connection with God. After our epic trip in Indochina, I realized many things, and slowly, as my relationship with God grows, so does the return of the desire for motherhood. As I learn more about God, I know how crucial the role of mothers is in His kingdom.

By twenty-seventeen, armed with my renewed hope and the practice of submission to the husband as outlined in the Bible, we made twenty-seventeen — the baby year. We laid low on our wanderings and made it a point to visit the obstetrician-gynecologist (OB) at the start of the year to have my PCOS re-assessed.

At this point, I have lost faith in the power of pills and medicine already, but the husband insisted. And since I was practicing submission, I gave pills a chance again. The OB told me to take the drugs for six months, and in the sixth month, I should return to have my PCOS checked. I was busy by June, so I returned in August. When the Doctor checked, the PCOS was still outstanding. I did bleed every month, but there was still no ovulation. The Doctor told me to return for a checkup, but I got busy. By September, I started a new journey in a new home — my third job.

Fresh from the disappointment comes the blessing of a new job. It was as if God was pacifying my heart by giving me my other desire — career growth. The frustration, forgotten, and the baby plan, overshadowed by ambitious career goals. But in all the blessings after blessings, I kept praying for God to take over. I let go of my control. When asked about the baby plan, instead of talking about my disappointment, I wondered every inquisitor to help me pray for the baby. Soon the baby prayer has become a routine. I got swamped, but I was unaware that in the background, the baby prayers were in the works.

Looking back at how I got obsessed with fitness because of sickness never fails to put me in self-reflection. I would often marvel at how God can turn a perceived test into a testimony. I have always been self-conscious, but when I had PCOS, the self-consciousness no longer matters.

Through the years, I decided to move more than I ever did and explore many exercises. I explored trekking starting at twenty-eleven and Zumba at twenty-fourteen. Muay Thai in twenty-fifteen. Yoga in twenty-seventeen. It's crazy how the more I write this book, the more I realize how "uniquely flawed" I am. Aside from my regular mental crisis, it appears that I had a traditional "fitness" pick each year too. It made me think if I did all those things because I am in a crisis, my situation could have gone way worse if not for the things I did. Which came first, the chicken or the egg?

However, in this pandemic, I have not been taking

care of my fitness at all. While I love the comforts that the work from home brings, it made me more workaholic than usual. As a person who enjoys doing things with another human being, I don't have anyone to encourage me to exercise at home. My husband can support me, but when it comes to exercise, I had to do it myself first.

I have many excuses for not doing "fitness" in quarantine, but it stops now. Hopefully, before I finish this book, I can report positive progress as, unlike the previous chapter, "fun," fitness is something that I can do at home despite the current circumstance. I need to overcome the barrier of "time" by choosing an activity that I can do at home and around our condo compound. Although my husband doesn't share my interest, I have to encourage him to do it as we are not getting any younger and being healthy is something we need to do for our baby girl.

CHAPTER EIGHT — FAITH IN THE THIRTIES

When the idea of drafting my debut book for my thirty-fifth birthday goal came up, I hesitated. It sounded crazy. I had already tried and failed before, so what made me think that I can finish it this time? The answer is nothing. Even in chapter eight, I still feel like I haven't made any progress at all. Each time I start a chapter, I would read back to make sure the idea connects. However, aside from its already an hour of fast reading time now, this chapter's topic makes me feel like it would stand on its own. It doesn't need any introduction. I should be okay.

But way before my faith, nothing is okay. The worst thing about not being okay without faith is that IT'S NOT OKAY, NOT TO BE OKAY. I am tired. That is the most frequent line you'd hear from me. Yeah. I feel so tired of everything that comprises my life. I often wonder how it feels not to be me.

Although I also think that maybe I'm not the only one in this shoe, yet I still hate the way my life is. I hate it so much; I want it to end.

Ending my life could be an answer. But I believe in hell, and I prefer not to burn in there forever. I love God, and I do thank Him every day for my blessings and occasionally, my problems too, and yet, I still want my life to end. As usual, I feel unfortunate, tired, and bored. I have been mailing some friends about the current problems, worries, and issues that have been bothering and bugging me at this point. I was waiting for their reply and advice when suddenly this idea came.

Why won't I make a worry blog instead of mailing friends? Because it could save a lot of my friend's time and advice. And also, sometimes I think my friends cannot relate to my problems at all. Reading and following their advice is not very helpful, I guess. Here comes SCREWORRIES. I couldn't think of a perfect name for the blog. But I like the sound of SCREW and WORRIES. I collected all my significant worries and started blogging.

Financial is my major dilemma. Whenever my boyfriend complains about how broke he is, I'm just burdened. I feel that it is my fault why he said so because he always picks the bill. It makes me gloomy, thinking I am excess baggage to him. I want it to stop by not making him pay; however, I couldn't afford much—no money to spend on extra snacks and outside dinners at all. My salary is for my brother's education and my mom's allowance at home. I am always broke, and it annoys me to hear him say that he's broke. He has thousands in his bank account. If he thinks he's broke having some, I wonder what he thinks of me. Probably, a beggar.

I have often wondered how it feels to have problems spending your salary because I'm the eldest child. My salary is for the family. It's sad to be jealous of others who don't have any responsibility to their families at all. As the eldest child of a single mom, I think it is my responsibility to uplift our societal status. I send my brother to school, and my mom stops working already. They all depend on me to live. At first, it is my joy to be of service to them. But as the years passed, I began to hate this responsibility. Often, I found myself wanting to end my life just to escape the burden. Thinking of what-ifs along the way and me failing out of expectations is my biggest fear.

On top of money and responsibility worries, I also have a confusing character. I easily camouflaged myself like a chameleon. With a group of saints, I would be mistaken for one. Put me on a pack of wolves, and I'll act like a wolf. Party people. Nerd. The Intellectuals. Fashionista. Boyish. The list goes on. Every so often, I wonder what group I truly belong to. I never feel like I truly belonged. I think I may have a multiple personality disorder. Furthermore, I always make it a point to ask people about their initial impressions of me. I do so because I don't grasp my authentic self. At school, from elementary to high school, I was a bully. Bossy. The Leader. Teacher's Pet. Last Say. Dictator. Independent. But at home, I am the most obedient child. I follow the rules, am very dependent, and you rarely hear me talk because I learn to scream in silence through my words. In my first year in college, I was very detached from people. I have my world. Selfish. Competitive. Grades were everything. Unfriendly. Judgmental. High hat. Demanding. Insensitive. However, somebody figured me out and melted my wall. Being useless as my Mom mainly did everything, I transferred my dependency to the invader. I thought of it as my ticket out of my crazy life. However, the invader got bored with the demanding princess. He left. It was scary at first, but then I learned to be single and ready to mingle. I have become the outgoing, bubbly, talkative, and friendly person most of my friends know now.

I'm no longer dependent on anyone. When I learned what it means to be free and fight, I was relentless. It makes me wonder whether people change behavior as quickly as I. Or am I the only one? Sporadically, there are days that I want to act coy and innocent, but during nighttime, I'd be the life of the party — wild, sensual, and daring. And I think I'm fantastic at both.

WHEN NOTHING FEELS RIGHT AT THIRTY-FIVE | 105

Image and reputation are everything to me. Being born of an unwed and a known playgirl mom is adamant. When I was young, I often heard people predicting my future. They would say that, just like my mom, I would get pregnant at an early age. It's tormenting to be living in an environment where everyone expects you to fall. I tried so hard to make people eat their predictions. I tried so hard to be perfect, to cut the trend of a traditional barrio thinking of "Like Mother, Like Daughter." It brought me enormous happiness when people talk of how I am blessed with both beauty and brains. I am also very refined and lady-like. I don't attend barrio discos, youth encounters, and all those sorts of youth gatherings.

Furthermore, I always stay at home. I created a perfect model image in our barrio. I often hear little children say that they want to be just like me when they grow up. When I went to college, I saw the world from a whole new perspective.

I abandoned my model image when someone made me realize how boring it is to be living at other's whim. I assumed a new me, but as soon as I got home, I never forgot to wear that barrio image again. That barrio image was my mask until I had my mid-twenty crises. I realized that it was crazy to be living in my mother's shadow.

I did get out of my mom's shadow, but the unfaithful genealogy takes over. My mom had two steady boyfriends when she had me. Both of them accepted paternity. So, it made me a daughter of two fathers. I didn't think it was weird before, but later I realized the sting of unfaithfulness. As I grew up, I have become so obsessed with my genealogy. It broke me more when I knew that it seems to be a common thing for the family's women. My grandmother left my grandfather to be with another man. My great-grandmother, my grandfather's mother, left her husband also to be with another man. That pattern could be traced back to my great-great-grandmother. It seems all the females of my root, including my mom, were practicing unfaithfulness. I don't know why I concluded that it is my responsibility to stop the unfaithfulness pattern. But as soon as I realized it, I then thought of ways not to follow their path. I vow that I would try my very best to be faithful. But even so, silly things would lead me to unfaithfulness. I had a severe three-year-old relationship before, but it ended because of a misunderstanding. I assumed that he was unfaithful. Due to my obsession with unfaithfulness, I have become an insecure and doubtful person.

Trade-off. Something for something. I don't think it is a case of an eye for an eye or a gift for a gift thing at first. I am just not that comfortable receiving something and not having the capacity to return the favor. If someone is nice to me, I couldn't sleep without thinking about ways to make them feel how grateful I am for their presence. I think it was sweet at first, but after some time, that behavior evolves. I soon concluded that maybe the golden rule is valid. Likewise, I start to care and care and care more, expecting that if I do so, people would care for me too. It took me a long time to realize not all people follow the golden rule, and not all are mindful of trade-offs. The period waiting, wanting, and expecting to care in almost the same way you cared for them was stressful. It makes my heart numb. But I didn't stop doing it. After all, though it's stressful, I find happiness in giving. But I don't understand why I am more at ease giving rather than receiving?

Then I Met Jesus.

My story wasn't theatrical. All the above worries were already out of the picture when it happened. I no longer have any deep trouble or trials. Not carrying any burden somehow made me feel like an outcast. Every time I will attend our Church gathering for the young professionals, the speakers would mention burdens that I don't already have. Occasionally, I would go out of the session wondering why I'm there.

But one time, the pastor mentioned my circumstance. John ten-ten says that the thief comes only to steal and kill and destroy, but Jesus says that they may have life and have it fully. I realized it was wrong to think that we only need God when we are down, but more so when we are in comfort because the enemy can easily steal our joy if we don't protect it. And aside from protecting what I have, God has been so good to me. Compared to before, my life hasn't been this good. I have been told that being who I am now is a miracle. I feel that God has purposely called me to be near Him. He has loved me so much that it's time I return Him all the glory and the love.

In July of twenty-seventeen, my relationship with Jesus grows more robust and stable. Back when I started, it was a struggle. I had many preoccupations. When I finally let God control my life, I realized how superfluous I was. I had many desires that weren't healthy. I was too full of myself, and though I kept telling how people's idea of me no longer affects me as it does in the past, it still actually did. Unconsciously, I had let other people dictate my life, like how it was when I was in our Barrio. I haven't been true to myself. Being with God exposed me. It made me look at my life with a new pair of eyes. I cringed at how I was before. I came to a point where I questioned everything, I hold dear, my values, and what I do. Not only that, but I got so down, I felt helpless and somehow almost give up on pursuing Him. I thought that if I didn't let Him in, I wouldn't have the confusion I was having.

But God is just remarkable. He was always there in

my struggles. He sent people to help me make it through, to help me to understand that I needed to face my fears, to re-visit my pains to appreciate everything He has blessed me with fully. I have always wanted to change, and each time I try, I fail. But with Him, change is an everyday thing. Even now, I am discovering things in myself that I never thought possible. Each time I read His word and worship Him, He tells me new things. There's never a dull moment with God. And every so often, I laugh out loud for the crazy things He puts in my head. Proof, this BOOK! God is now my best friend. Now, decisions made are not entirely mine alone. I listened to what He says and, in constant prayer, that He will be patient with me always.

I learned that God is spectacular, loving, and He talks to us every day. We just didn't have the time to listen to Him. I always thought that doing good things is my ticket to salvation. Now, I know that His grace already saves us. Our salvation is not something we work for. It's a gift from God. We need to open the facility and receive it. But not because we are already saved that we stop doing good. Obedience to Him is part of our duty as His children. If we honor our earthly father, who is just with us for a time, we should keep our great Father, who will be with us for eternity. I learned that He is very merciful and that no matter how dirty we think we are, God can cleanse us as white as snow. Everything is possible with Him.

It's never too late to come to Him. His doors are always open for those who are willing. Nothing can satisfy us more than His love and comforts. God sees everyone equally. No rich, no poor. No sound, no sinners. In His eyes, we are all His beloved children.

I didn't significantly change when I accepted Jesus as my personal Lord and savior. My changes were overwhelming, but most of them are inner changes. Before I had God, I was already good. I didn't have any ungodly physicality. My main difference was I have become picky. I now favor the right relationships. Unlike before where I try to befriend everyone, now I value my words and story. I am learning the art of listening more than talking. Being alone is not at all scary and weird. I have also known not to force myself on people and forced them on me. And have taught me to stay away from the poisons of social media. I still share, but not as much as before. And these days, I noticed how I have become less bored. I have learned how to appreciate downtimes. Spending the weekend at home is primarily welcome nowadays.

My thirty-fifth birthday is a significant milestone as it is not only my halfway to the thirties but is also my marker. I met Jesus in April of twenty-sixteen, which, if you noticed, is always the start of my birthday crisis. I still have problems sporadically but unlike in my twenties, having my faith is an assurance that I can bounce back higher from where I slumped.

Despite being new, I got involved with the church and served two ministries. I was cautious not to be consumed with the tasks to forget my primary purpose. Though I started slow and did not push myself too hard, I was satisfied. My main goal was to serve the Lord and not people. I find mentors for my walk with God. Being mentored was a first for me. I was not comfortable being mentored, as I work best learning the ropes on my own. However, I have learned that to pursue a more significant role in the future, and I need other people. When I started serving two ministries in the twenty-seventeen, I thought it was crazy. However, when God answered my prayer of Unyara Seresa, I knew that God was preparing me for her. I was fully equipped and ready when she came at Thirty-two.

I was so consumed with the relationship that I regularly attended church services from Sunday to work-week services. Likewise, I loved Bible Study and looked forward to the sessions. I hungered to listen and communicate with God and make my daily devotional our particular time when God can tell me anything. Reminiscing on how busy I was with church stuff pre-pandemic always warms my heart. Not because I miss it, but because it makes me feel satisfied that I did what I could when I had the time.

Serving God is thoroughly unique in the time of

quarantine. Despite the social distancing and the emotional stress brought by being indoors, I never stop sharing how Jesus made me better. And that they shouldn't let initial hesitations prevent them from knowing Him more.

As humans, we are very eager to try other things, but when it comes to the Lord, we are always hesitant. Nothing is more important than our relationship with God. The items in this world are temporary. God is permanent. Let's store endless treasures, not temporary ones. Give Jesus a chance to show you how to live louder with Him.

Speaking life and living louder for God's purpose has become my drive. Sometimes, in the chaos of every day, we forget that we are made for a bigger purpose other than nitpicking or concerning ourselves with worldly woes. Making decisions was no longer automatic for me. I have to pray for it.

Everything needs to be prayed for. Leading people has become more challenging since I wanted to give them freedom as Jesus did. He never forced people to follow Him. People just follow Him. Although I'm not forcing people to follow me by force, I think I might have been unconsciously forcing them to follow me because I am kind and friendly. I love it that everywhere I go, I draw people together. Connecting like-minded individuals and seeing people become good friends makes me happy, but I don't want it to stop there. I should learn to create groups that will continue without me.

Aside from that, I make sure I listen to God more to align my plans to His. God is accountable to my goals too. And the more I accept new things, the more I would make it harder to make Him my priority. That's why agreeing to write the book and announcing it is crazy, but now you know where I got my bravery from.

The Godless heart of my twenties brought me pain as each time I had pre-birthday mental meltdowns; I don't have a relationship with Jesus, who puts me in perspective. The birthdays in my thirties were different. I have welcomed the thirties on a life-changing multi-country trip that humbled me. The success of my thirtieth birthday trip to Indochina made me realize how crazy my social media habits are. I have finally learned to be genuinely confident without the need for people's approval.

At thirty-one, I achieved my goal of celebrating my birthday on an outreach. Along with five of my friends, we brought food to the mental center where my mom was confined when diagnosed with Bipolar Disorder. As a child, I would often dream of celebrating a birthday with those in need. I always have a hunger to give and for those in need, but in my thirties, giving is an everyday thing. I want to give back to society and those around me regularly. On the last payday, I started doing random acts of kindness to my team by surprising one of them with food. I want to avoid saying how my tithes help me with my finances, but I feel more comfortable with my finances, knowing I have given to God what's His in the first place.

Thirty-two was the defining moment of my thirties because I spent my birthday on bump shoots. There was nothing more that could make me happier, knowing that God has given me the miracle of Unyara in the year that I unknowingly planned for it. I saw a timeline made in twenty-ten where I had thirty-two as the year to get pregnant. I also have a post where I wished to do a bump shoot at thirty-two.

Having the time of my life at thirty-two with my firstborn was remarkable. My birthday at thirty-three was toned-down because we planned Unyara's first birthday. However, my very awesome brother organized a surprise party. The party is already good, but he invited my aunt from abroad to surprise me. It was super spectacular that knowing he will fly to the United States two days after my birthday felt a little less painful. Double surprise, eh?

And then a birthday at thirty-four in quarantine. It probably is my most uneventful birthday, but God planted the idea of a podcast in my head. Even now, as I was thinking about the podcast, my heart would swell in reverence to the God who made it happen. I haven't been podcasting lately, but as soon as I'm done with this book, I surely will.

Counting down to my thirty-fourth birthday with a podcast is a distant memory now. I remembered how I look forward to my mid-thirties while writing about it. Pre-birthday mental meltdown kept me thinking about how to celebrate differently in quarantine. Birthdays have always been a thing, but for the last three birthdays, after the epic thirtieth birthday celebrated on a two-week four-country escape in Indochina, I just settled with a tone-down celebration.

However, the quarantine made me miss many people, and I thought my birthday would be an excellent excuse to gather online, but as I evaluated the plan more, I just froze. My intentions are good, but picking without any reason is just better. If five months into the quarantine didn't move people into an online zoom catch-up, meeting for a birthday wouldn't make a difference.

So instead of focusing my energy on creating that zoom catch-up, I have used my power to start my podcast. I had tons of fun talking on the podcast. It makes me feel a certain kind of exhilaration every time I listen to myself on record.

I celebrated my birthday on the podcast. After a month of podcasting, a lot has happened. Still, if there's one thing that I love about my relationship with Christ, it is the understanding that I am only a limited human despite the unlimited source of energy in Him. To keep things together, the first order of business is to put God first and let Him do the rest.

Thankfully, I have some time and inspiration. After a week from my last podcast, I remembered missing Sunday's reflection. The plan was to do a back-to-back podcast of Sunday services. However, the week was heavy for me physically, but so grateful that God was with me spiritually. I have recovered because of my Bible devotional, and each time, God's assurance and promises were heartwarming.

I planned well with the first few episodes, but midway, I realized that I'd survive with no prior preparations. Episodes one to six were done between one- and three-days intervals, which means that on weeknights, I still have some breathing space. Sundays were also free days, but starting mid-August, it got crazy busy due to a work deployment on the twenty-second. Because the working week and some Saturdays are hectic, Sunday was the only time to rest. It was only by God's grace that on the sixteenth of August, I was able to podcast the Sunday reflection.

The week of my birthday was the busiest. It has taken a toll on me physically, emotionally, and spiritually. Two days before my birthday, I received news that a close friend died, on top of learning that my manager's last day is a day after my birthday. The plan to take a day off on my birthday was canceled because things at work were bleak. I was torn between mourning and celebrating, to appreciating. August seventeen to August twenty-eight was a blur. I can narrate what happens to me day by day, but now I can survive — only by His grace. That's only the circumstances. I haven't mentioned yet that while these crazy things are happening to me, something is happening within me.

My last menstruation was in May. I saw the signs that my PCOS is back, but I didn't have time to notice it until the thirty-first of July; the husband pointed out that my "dandruff" looks terrible. It was an understatement, though. It's way worse. Since the thirty-first of July, I have been recording the progress of my "dandruff," which turns out to be a "Psoriasis," diagnosed in September.

It was crazy how I hadn't noticed that it was that bad. Thankful to my husband, who always kept me in check. Without his intervention, I wonder where it would lead. Psoriasis is an immune system dysfunction, like PCOS; it's better to manage through lifestyle.

My faith in God has changed things for me. It continuously does so even as I'm writing this book. It is very overwhelming to know that, despite our sinful nature. We are loved. Let me close this chapter with a post from my blog.

An Unexpected Encounter

After staying indoors for most of the week, I rode with my husband to IT Park. He had Saturday work, and I had a life group meetup. Since the rally is still at four in the afternoon, I brought my laptop, so I could finally finish Unyara's First Birthday Planning in Excel. But God had another plan in mind. Armed with my favorite honey calamansi from Serenitea, I went to look for a seat. The place was crowded. I knew someone from my bible study group. She looked busy, so I thought of sitting away from her, so I don't disturb her with my chatter. However, the only set available was beside her.

I tried not to bother her. I don't know her that much too, but I remembered I saw her at my brother's master's graduation, so I asked how she is, where she's currently working, and if she's now practicing her profession. That kicked off our exchange. She was having some pre-occupations about God's plan for her life now. She turns between waiting on Him or going ahead with her plans. Should she stay or push herself? There was a lot in her head. It seems like she needed someone to talk to. Oh well, I thought, Unyara's planning can wait.

Share your God's story. You never know who you inspire through it. When I was still using FB messenger, I sometimes shared my posts on our chat group. It was sort of a one-way share only, just like with my other channels. Unlike before, I don't expect people to read, but I still put it out there anyway. Nothing was taken from me when I share, and it's up to them to read and celebrate God's goodness through my experience. It turns out she reads the posts.

We jumped from topic to topic but mostly centered on God's hand in my life before I was even a Christian. It was some sort of compressed version of Kresia version 3.0! From the controlling-overly-insecure-people-pleasing-victim-of-fate-envious-brat to miss-positivity-fun-obsessed-social-media-queen to now. God is always there. He is always present, but because we are too occupied with being self-reliant, we often miss His voice reminding us of His plans. God is as involved in our lives as we are. Our plans are good, but when it is aligned to His, it is powerful.

There's nothing wrong with planning for our lives, but it is a better practice to consult or wait for God's approval. It's funny how we often seek the world's approval but not God's. We often burden ourselves with so much "what would people think's that instead of appreciating what God had blessed us so far, we still whine for more.

There is so much that God can do with our lives if we let go and let Him. Living in a relationship with Him is so much better. It is not pure happiness always, but you know that whenever trials come, He is teaching you something. Just like in a worldly relationship with your significant other, there are moments of bliss and torment, but at the end of the day, you know it is for the relationship's growth. Contentment at its finest. When you are in the center of God's plans, everything can be disturbingly bland. There's not much action. You feel that God is not with you anymore because He is busy fixing others but knows God is still with you. Keep praying and communicating with Him no matter what season you are in. In the season of waiting, learn to be patient and be mindful of the lessons that He is teaching you.

Waiting can be a bum but know that He lets you wait for a reason. I wish I'd known this when I was having a mid-twenty crisis. It would have been so much better to have lived through that time without drama. But it is evident how He looks out for me by giving me a boyfriend. Sometimes, in our struggle, we tend to suffer with it independently. It doesn't have to be. Look and find the people God strategically put in your life to help you through it. Settle and be content but be always ready for something new.

My resignation from my previous company was a total shock to me. I thought I wasn't ready, but it was only at the end that I realized that God did the necessary preparations for me. There are things in our life that we don't understand why we are doing it and for what purpose. When I decided to resign from my ambassadorship and re-align the women's leadership strategy, I thought I was doing it for the baby. It wasn't. God made me do it because He wanted me to transfer. I never asked for a new job, but God sees I needed the promotion. He sees that I deserved something better and has prepared me for Unyara.

All things will work out in the end according to God's plans for your life. You might be having a hard time now; check if you listen to God's voice. If you are, then there's nothing to worry about. Keep on having that conversation with Him and be open to anything. And while you're waiting for your very own miracle, don't forget to SPEAK LIFE to everyone you encounter. We are not here on earth for ourselves only. God put us here for a purpose. Let us continue to LIVE LOUDER for Him, so will be His very own disciple to those who are deaf to His words yet. Because at the end of the day, we are not building a future in this temporary place. Let's collect the true wealth!

CHAPTER NINE — LIFE OF FAITH

As a person, I regularly check how I grew through the years. The very reason for my social media posts is to document my life to look back at everything when I'm old and grey. Unfortunately, when my relationship with Christ grew, I realized how twisted my reasons were and that some people who don't matter may have judged my motives because of my oversharing. And as the years go by, I find it harder to keep up with the social media noises. Nowadays, not logging in to social media every day is no longer a surprise. I can sometimes forget my cell phone the whole day. Find myself thriving more in this pandemic, including losing my social media habits. Furthermore, for the first time, this twenty-twenty-one, I have been very faithful with giving tithes and have saved more money than I ever did.

In the past few days, I spent some time writing

on my blog again. I initially wanted to do a podcast, but the rain prevented it. Now that I'm back to writing, I realized that I missed the feels too. One big difference between writing and speaking is that I enjoy reading about what I've written and built the following paragraphs on top of what I wrote. For podcasting, everything is very raw— no going-backs and edits. Despite the significant differences, I think both can do good for me. After blogging, Unyara demanded some time, so I had to stop doing it. When I returned from the Unyara time, I felt it would be better not to continue what I started doing — create a plan for the following weeks leading up to my thirty-fifth birthday on the twentieth of August. I picked up a different task from the never-ending list of life organizing and assessments — update Unyara's timeline and create our Migo&Miga timeline. To my surprise, I partly did Unyara's timeline already. The "YouTube" sheet puts me in awe as it already has the links to all the Unyara items placed at "Life with Kring TV." I can't believe how I have forgotten that I have already started. I continued creating our timeline, which was done already, but I forgot the filename. Instead of looking for it, I started a new one. While looking back through Migo and I's years, I separated our timeline per relationship milestone. When I searched for it, I read many posts from LifeHack.org that led me to do a "Life Assessment."

> "Everything you've ever wanted is on the other side of fear." — George Addair

I had second thoughts of doing the life assessment as I fear knowing where I stand. But as George Addair said, everything you've ever wanted is on the other side of fear. So, despite it, I answered the assessment as truthfully as I could. Instead of feeling disappointed, I felt happier with the result. I never thought I'd be at sixty-five percent fulfillment. It may seem low, but at least I didn't fall beyond fifty. It made me happier to realize that I lack thirty-five to a hundred. The percentage is significant considering I'll be thirty-five in a few days. Thinking how I could increase to thirty-five in another thirty-five years makes my heart race.

Among the thousand posts on my blog, the word "fulfilled" is only mentioned in eleven blogs. When I skimmed through it, I'm in awe at what I have found. The first entry was on twenty-eleven. The year that I declared that I had a mid-twenty crisis. It's in April, too, where most of my yearly meltdown begins.

I am at a loss for the many things that need to be done. Day by day, something just pops in and sways me away from my goals. Each day, I arrived home feeling empty for goals unmet. Every day, my "to-do" lists keep growing. I wonder when that list will be emptied.

I'm a little scared to set goals now because I'm unsure if I can achieve them. Everything seems uncontrollable, and I'm not too fond of it. I hate everything in this post except one thing. That one special feeling keeps me motivated every day. It fueled me to keep working hard and forget unfulfilled goals' anxiety. I'm glad this feeling exists because I wonder what else I could do to survive if it isn't.

Getting into the brain of the twenty-four-year-old me who was about to have a mid-twenty crisis gives me mixed emotions. Sad because I had to experience it but happy because, despite the craziness, I had survived. There are two more posts from twenty-eleven. Another one in twenty-twelve titled "Where to Go from Here?"

I still don't know. But some things are sure; I won't stop seeing places, trekking mountains, mingling with people, and, of course, sharing the love. Sometimes, depression visits me. Bringing all those unfulfilled dreams I once held dear dreams mostly for my family. I did not stop dreaming for them. I choose not to kill myself, trying too hard to be the person my family wanted me to be. It's a painful learning process. How could you stop doing something when you've been doing it too long, it becomes a habit? But it's time that I dream for myself. I'm not getting any younger. I should seriously consider what I want to do for the rest of my life. And that's my ultimate dilemma. At this point, I'm not sure where to go from here. A shameful little secret, I forced someone to pick the decision for me. I just can't decide for myself. Grateful that someone was sensible enough to realize my desperation. While I'm happy that he could talk sense into me, now I'm back to where I've always been-LOST! Where do I go from here? Sadly, I don't know yet. I'm waiting for the universe to push me somewhere.

It must have sucked not knowing where to go and feeling like you don't have the power to make your choice. Perhaps the reason there was no entry since the last post in twenty-twelve is that I may have spent the next five years finding my direction and searching for fulfillment. I shared the journey in the previous chapters of this book. I thought that a fulfilled life could be achieved through travel, self-love, trek, and other things. However, while those give me fulfillment, they were short-lived until I met Jesus in twenty-seventeen.

During one of my Bible Study Thursdays in twenty-seventeen, the chapter lesson is titled "God Fulfills His promise." That lesson aims to remind us to trust God to always protect us. Despite how fickle our faith in Him is, just like Abraham, God will always come to our rescue. At the end of everything, it is not how faithful we are but how trustworthy He is. His purpose is the only purpose that would be fulfilled and nothing else. All we need to do is simply rely on Him, not putting matters into our hands.

Of the many lessons learned from that session, "God Fulfills His promise" is what struck me most. Lots of things have been happening to me. And despite God's faithfulness in my life, when things look bleak, I would automatically revert to my worldly self — thinking more of what other people think and not what God is telling me.

Since leaving my comfort zone in August of twenty-seventeen, I was ushered into a journey of mixed emotions. I want to change my attitude from miss congeniality to being just part of the crowd. The doubt of thinking about other people too much when it's not necessary. The realization that I have been growing horizontally in faith, focusing more on my relationship with people instead of focusing on my relationship with Christ. All of it was rooted in how badly I care for people. It's not wrong to watch with a limit. Unfortunately, the limit doesn't seem to exist in my vocabulary. The topic was a timely reminder of how imbalanced my life was. And taking a break from people and my Facebook habit is just what I needed. I should focus on what He calls me to do and not on the unnecessary pressures of my attachment to the world.

The five years from the start of my mid-twenty crisis until the entry to my thirties seemed like the best time of my life when I started writing this book. In twenty-thirteen, I had my first international trip abroad. We got engaged in twenty-fourteen, married in twenty-fifteen, and a multi-celebration in twenty sixteen. We had our first international trip as a couple on our first wedding anniversary, celebrated my thirtieth birthday on a multi-country trip to Indochina, and had our first car. Twenty-seventeen doesn't seem to have anything. It was the year that we decided to cancel all our fun to focus on the baby. But now, as I am collecting the pieces like puzzles on a giant jigsaw puzzle of life, I realized that twenty-seventeen is the last piece. No matter how beautiful the rest of the other parts, the fulfilled life that I longed to have would not be complete without it.

As a person who thrives in action, the rest imposed on twenty-seventeen feels like a limitation. However, if not for that rest, I wouldn't have the disturbingly profound experience at our Church's Recharge Camp that melted my pride to pray for the baby. After an overwhelming life-changing experience, just like the multi-country trip in Indochina, the pressure to write goes first before the urge to share. I feel that talking about it would jeopardize the memory-making me feel less compelled to write. And being me, not writing is a problem. You see, I'm a "Dory." I quickly forgot things. To remember, I need something to remind me, thus the need to take pictures of everything and write a blog after. My blogs exist mainly for me, but it makes me happy when my story can inspire others. It warms my heart every time I got messages from people inspired by my post. And lately, I make it a point to let others know if I was inspired by their post.

After the camp, the husband picked me up. There was a slight misunderstanding. He was hangry (hungry and angry), but thanks to my just recharged self, it was turned around. We then had a fantastic talk at our favorite burger place in the city — Burger Joint. Just like I said, I wanted to avoid talking. It wasn't planned. I wasn't thinking of sharing. He was all supportive in my pursuits, but there's just something in him that makes me uneasy. I was afraid that if I share with him my experience, because of how he is towards my newfound glory in God, instead of magnifying what I felt, he'll do the opposite. I was wrong.

It started awkwardly. Every time we are away from each other, once we are reunited, I will begin art talking nonstop about everything. But that time, I was just silent. I asked him what he has been doing while I'm away instead. He answered silently. After a while, he asked, "How was it?". I paused. I didn't expect him to ask. Likewise, I wasn't planning to share either. "Didn't you see my Facebook post?" I answered. He said no and hadn't had time to check when he woke up from the nap. I opened my phone and showed him my recently posted collage of the incredible people I met at the camp. I went to the camp alone, not thinking it is a problem because wherever I go, I just easily fit in. Besides, it wasn't the people that I'm interested in. I wanted to know God more, but what happened was, I knew Him more by the people I got to interact with.

I am always the girl with a plan, but I wasn't planning to be Miss Congeniality like usual. It just happened, as if the Lord is telling me to let my light shine. Since I started pursuing Jesus, I acquired a new peace within me. It affected the way I interact with others was. Before, I always made it a point to create a wave of positivity, be extra animated or chatty. Instead of doing it right away, I observed the mood first. This change has earned me some comments on the first few days since I received Jesus. People were asking how I was. They asked if I'm going through something since I'm not as energetic as usual. I just smiled through the comments. Next time I'll say, "Yes, I'm going through something big. Jesus now lives in me."

Back to the camp (oh me, easily distracted even in writing), I noticed that most people were meek. I have only known a few who had a ready smile and high spirits. It seems they are hesitant or maybe observing too. It made me uneasy. I didn't plan to unleash the sunny-sunshine-me as I want to be just part of the crowd, but then the Lord told me to soak in and let my light show. But somehow, a part of me had regrets about why I had to be what I always am. Yet, a more significant part was triumphant because I could connect to more people apart from my group. My only hope is that I could touch their lives positively. They will remember how I make them feel despite how I seem to do all the talking because I was trying too hard not to talk but listen more instead.

I was with ten very diverse individuals in different seasons of life. I'm with a couple, two mothers, one other wife aside from me, one teenager, and four singles. Despite that, it didn't hinder us from connecting, even though we have an American groupmate compelling us to speak English.

I had a different set of people as roommates. They were a mixture of various characters. We were eight. There were two teen girls, and the rest were adults. We were primarily busy, but every time we got together in the room, conversations flowed freely. The stories I've learned from my group and my roommates were priceless, from unbelieving husbands to ghost stories to miracles to relationships and everything under the sun. Listening to each of their testimonies helps me evaluate my faith in God and be more in love with how He is. The Lord has done marvelous work in their lives. We glorify God's name in our conversations.

Every session starts with worship, but the night sessions were the best. The two nights of prayer made me realize just how little my faith in God was. I never really prayed in specifics. It wasn't terrible since, at that point, I never really had anything to pray for. That's what I thought. But as I was getting into the mood of worship, with all my inhibitions away, my desire surfaced. When I started praying aloud and humble myself before God, I remembered my heart's desire. God's presence exposes what I felt. I placed my PCOS (Polycystic Ovarian Syndrome) struggles and how they had affected my desire to have a child. He made me realize that aside from PCOS, what hinders me from praying hard for a child is my childhood experiences from being born to a teenage and abusive mother. I was afraid of my childhood trauma. Yes, I have forgiven Mom for everything she did to me, but the remnants of what I've been through have kept me paranoid. I feel it would be better not to end up like her. I'm terrified that I'll never be a good mother.

And as my reflection got deeper and deeper, aside from PCOS and the childhood trauma, what kept me from wanting to have children is myself. The harsh environment and my struggles have made me love myself above everyone else. That self-love has been my shield and weapon. It keeps me from tearing myself apart. I'm afraid that if I bore children, I will forget myself. And if I do, will I still be the same? Can I forget myself? What if I can't? What if I'll just resent the child? And more what-ifs. The fear froze me and almost made me blackout. And then I remembered a group mate's words; perfect love casts out all fear. And yes, it does.

Aside from new friends and knowing God more, the greatest gift I received from the camp is direction. I'm primarily content and comfortable with my life, though not a bad thing; I was very hesitant to embrace the next best thing — motherhood. This new direction will be hard; it is not guaranteed if it is God's purpose for me, but I am giving it a chance. Recharge twenty-seventeen was so overwhelmingly incredible that it left me profoundly disturbed, in a good way.

I ended my twenty-twelve, looking for direction everywhere but with God. After God's leading during our Church's camp to the path of motherhood, I was still unsure. It's one thing to pray, but at the back of my mind was a human limitation. Instead of focusing on the restriction, I trusted in God more by listening and connecting to him more. I started twenty-seventeen with nothing but closed it out with everything.

After the camp in April, the months that followed were the busiest that I have ever been, but despite that, I had the peace of God. In one of my times with God, my life verse was given.

"Humble yourselves, therefore, under God's mighty hand, that he may lift you in due time." — 1 Peter 5:6 NIV

"Write to share," not "Write to impress," I told a friend. Writing in a public journal is just about those two, I think. These passing days, I realized another — "Do not write if you don't feel like writing." While feelings are mostly what fuels me to do things, and so far, I have been doing good following it, I realized relying on my emotions is no good. It's very unsustainable. To rely on the feelings of a very emotional and volatile being is crazy. It is also prideful.

But to whom should I rely upon? To rely on people or anything is something I'm not superb at. Over the years, there is only one person that I have complete confidence in. Myself. I sometimes remember to pray that I would transfer this confidence into stability and will never fail, EVER. Yet despite all the pursuits and the efforts, when the going gets tough, I would always find myself reverting to the old habits — relying on myself instead of God.

This habit is keeping me very guilty. It just shows how little my faith in Him is and how immense my pride is. My first recharge camp has stirred and shook me, it lit a fire inside, but I am at a loss as to how I can keep the fire burning without relying on my strength but His. I have been praying for a life verse. I had my list, but God wanted another. And being me, I reasoned why it's not my verse.

Yet after a Tuesday prayer at our Church, while I am writing, something tells me that what I want doesn't matter. The only thing that matters is His. I need strength, patience, and all the fruits of the spirit, but my pride always gets in the way. Our Pastor talked about praying as if you have already received it. I started praying, but I was very self-conscious and distracted. I prayed for a child, but then a thought came, are you sure you want it? Then everything started falling apart.

After much thought, deeply introspective, and a post, I have concluded that a child shouldn't be my prayer. My prayer should be to humble myself in God's hand. If I deepened my relationship with Him, I would hear His voice despite the loudness of everything in my life. The goal is not to revert to my old habit every time the going gets tough. I have been praying the wrong prayer. He made me realize what I want in the recharge camp, but today, I am reminded that my want does not matter. What matters most is Him. My mountains will not move if I don't have FAITH. And faith does not come cheap. To have faith is to believe; to believe is to humble under His mighty power, to recognize that I am nothing without Him.

CHAPTER TEN– PRODUCT OF FAITH

Reading from my blog, my earliest post mentioning pregnancy is on the fifth of October, twenty-eleven. I wrote about the excitement of writing about my family soon — the family I'll have with the then-boyfriend-now-husband. It just warms my heart to realize that my yesteryear's thoughts about posting details for my wedding and pregnancy are no longer just posts but a reality. The greatest of them all is that on the sixth of October twenty-eighteen, seven years after I first wrote the word "pregnancy," God gave us Unyara. From then on, I never stopped blabbering about her brilliance and wittiness, the very words that I wrote seven years ago.

Whenever the number seven appears in my life, it feels like God's personal love letter. In Scripture, the significance of the number seven is completion and perfection; Genesis tells us that God created the heavens and the Earth in six days, and, upon completion, God rested on the seventh day. Completion and perfection are the reminders that God revealed to me when she gave Unyara, seven years after I desired for her. The story of Unyara happened way before the actual pregnancy. I later learned that when you are aligned with God's will for your life, everything flows and is provided for. God always gave provision before the vision. All you must do is obey.

On the tenth of July, twenty-seventeen, an agent texted me about a job I didn't apply for. It took me a while to reply to countless reasons I don't need the job. Busy. No internet. It has been a while since I used the hiring skill. Contented and more reasons why I don't need a new job but now that I am looking back at that moment, I realized that if God works, your hesitations, doubts, and incapacity won't matter. You only must let Him lead. His will, your obedience. That's it.

Reading back at the text message history, I was amazed at how the conversation progressed. I could only mutter "Haba ng hair" to myself. "Haba ng hair" is a Pinoy phrase that you say when people are overconfident. Me already. Child of God, indeed.

In the seventh month on my team, four days before the eight months of my third job, reading back entries at our internal blog made me emotional and awed by God's goodness. In the background of it all was His promise in Isaiah 41:10.

> So do not fear, for I am with you; do not be dismayed, for I am your God. I will strengthen you and help you; I will uphold you with my righteous right hand. — Isaiah 41:10.

My plan was good, but God's was pure perfection. It's as if Joseph the dreamer's life is unfolding before my very eyes. Sold into slavery by his jealous brothers, he rose to become vizier, the second most powerful man in Egypt next to Pharaoh. His presence and office caused Israel to leave Canaan and settle in Egypt.

I might not have been sold to slavery, but my childhood was chaotic and full of misery. Being born to a teenage mom, growing up, I carried the burden of the saying, "Like mother, like daughter." No matter what I do, people won't stop judging me for my parent's fault. But instead of living up to their worst expectation, I rose to become the person they never thought I could be. Yet even with my successes, the hatred that I felt for those people who made me think less of myself stayed and scarred me, making me overly narcissistic to cover up the pains and emptiness. Then God came and rescued me from self-sabotage. When God came, He healed everything. Now, I am a new person settling in the place where God wanted me to be.

The transition from my second job to my current

job feels like I'm living from the Land of Comfort Zone to a Land of Doom. No one knew of my transfer but God. It was a mystery even to me. People call it craziness to leave the place where I have been blessed and comfortable to a place of uncertainty and stress. They predicted my doom, but I trusted in God's words and obeyed.

> Observe what the Lord your God requires: Walk in obedience to him, and keep his decrees and commands, his laws, and regulations, as written in the Law of Moses. Do this so that you may prosper in all you do and wherever you go. — Kings 2:3.

My obedience brought forth a manifold of blessings. God brought me to a remarkable team, led me to a Godly manager and an environment where I could continue to shine my Jesus light. But the best of the bests is the miracle of Unyara Teresa, my firstborn. I remembered how people teased that if I transfer, it would be harder for the baby to come. I teased back that my baby is a dragon and will only come under fire. It never fails to make me smile every time I remember the joke. God must have prepared my heart at that point to be able to say it aloud.

What others thought of the Land of Doom has become my paradise. God's favors overwhelmed. Every day, I am thankful for His guidance and in constant awe of His perfect plans. It still makes my heart flutter whenever I am reminded that we knew about the pregnancy in the first session of the couple ministry that I prayed about. My heart skipped to realized that God has been preparing me for motherhood all along. He wanted me to enjoy pregnancy and cherish the moments with my little one on four-month maternity leave, so He processed my transfer. My third job has four-month maternity as part of the benefits. My second job doesn't have it. God wanted me to celebrate with a bang on my thirty-second birthday as well, so He had timed Unyara's age in the tummy to be at week thirty-two on the day of the celebration. And because I am His favored, spoiled brat child who loves to celebrate anniversaries more than anything, He had to pick October as Unyara's birth month because it is my anniversary month on the team. God knows how to make His child happy. Who wouldn't obey a Father like that? He is just the absolute best!!!

My new company is proof that God's plans are always better than mine. My team is a product of prayers and good influences. Unyara is a testament to His faithfulness and love. My life is all for His glory.

Talking about Unyara leads me back to God and I's meet cute. February of twenty-sixteen, I was misled by a friend into attending a Church's young adult gathering for the first time. It has been a while since she actively invited me, but I always had reasons why can't. In one instance, she got creative and had me at the "Relationship" topic. And like maybe every reluctant first-timer at a Christian gathering, worship weirded me out.

I saw people raising their hands, and some were crying while singing. It was so new that I was convinced I'm in the wrong place. But because I love my friend, I stayed until the end. I thought that was it. What I didn't know was God's plan for me.

Two months have quickly passed, and though the first time has left a bitter taste, God put a desire for a second try. This time I brought a friend. With the friend who invited me, I attended a second time on the twentieth of April, twenty-sixteen. Since then, every Wednesday has become a time for God's revelation and a change of heart.

What has become a Wednesday thing soon became an everyday habit as I yearned for God's presence and guidance more? Growing up, I never really had any mentor and had little desire to be mentored. Self-confidence and self-reliance were two of my strengths. But as my relationship with God grew, He slowly peeled my coverings one by one until I was fully exposed and vulnerable.

Before God, I am a strong woman born out of the many struggles that I have won. Strong-willed and believes nothing is impossible if I put my heart into it. I care much about how people think of me. Narcissistic and self-absorbed, as if the world revolves around me.

When God came, He showed me how pointless my life has been. I was greedy and taking all the glory for everything that He has blessed me with. Instead of pointing back the glory to Him, I accumulated everything and became prideful. Because I was too full of myself, there was no room for God to expand me. I was stuck. Yet, God being God, He has ways in realigning us to His plans. But only if we allow Him to. We were all given free will. Like others, free will has become the roadblock to my relationship with Him. But God was patient. He was relentless in winning me over.

The first lesson that God taught me was surrender. To forget everything, I thought about myself and allowed Him to make me the person He wanted me to be. He wanted me to empty myself in surrender so that He could work on my emptiness. The struggle was real!

God wanted me to turn self-confidence into God-confidence. Control and confidence were the building blocks of who I was. When God asked for surrender, I panicked. There was so much in my life that is holding me back. God wants me to let it go. In my mind was the fear that if I do, everything will break. My first test was my marriage.

At Overflow — the young adult ministry every Wednesday focused on helping the joiners on three things: Relationship, Career, and Ministry. Every time the topic was finding the one, I would automatically thank Him for giving me God's best, even if I don't have any idea what God's best was then. Yet, even in my gratefulness, I haven't completely let go of my control towards the husband. I was always fearful that if I were to lose control, some sneaky flirty innocent-looking friendly cheat would ruin what we had, and I would blame myself for not being cautious.

But God had other ideas. He knew what I was afraid of. The early months of my journey as a neophyte-born again Christian strain our marriage. As I grew deeper in my relationship with God, I have become more and more judgmental towards other people. The husband struggled because of my disobedience. Instead of obeying God to let go of my control, I have become more controlling towards the husband as I label people he is associated with.

It was a crazy time, but God was patient. He waited until I learned the fruit of my disobedience. Due to my instability, I mired our once-happy marriage with inconsistencies. From the supportive husband of a Christian wife, he withdrew and became unresponsive. With no one else to go and ask for counsel, God put surrender once again on the table. I had no choice but to. From that day on, God showed me that no marriage problem is formidable in His hands. God wrote our marriage in His book; I trusted that He would do everything in His power to keep it pure.

From marriage, God slowly revisited all areas of my life that I needed to surrender and let go of control. Each process was different, but every time, I am taught the value of relying on Him more than myself. I may have survived on self-confidence for so long, but to move forward, God-confidence was the key. And if ever you asked yourself why you're stuck on where you are now? Maybe you have relied on your own too much. It's time you rely on God too.

From the marriage woes, God moved on to my career. There was a restlessness in my heart. I was happy, but something was missing. Twenty-seventeen was the baby year, but God had other plans.

Every year was a blessing, but twenty-sixteen was a bang. We traveled to four countries in Indochina as a welcome to my thirties in August and had our first car by November. Twenty-seventeen was the baby year, but God made it a provision year, preparing for the baby instead. In July of twenty-seventeen, God expanded and gave me a new career. Something that I have been waiting for but too scared to pursue.

In my pursuit to live the life I thought I needed to have; I forgot my relationship with God. Each year, I dreamed of material things and neglected the main point of my existence, to glorify God in whatever I do. Things do not simply happen because of our will, but a big God causes things to happen. Unyara is not an accident or a coincidence. God made things possible, and the only thing that God required from me is obedience.

People who knew about my polycystic ovarian syndrome and the effects that it has on my fertility asked what I did to get pregnant. Foolish me tried to level up with them by explaining the human things that I did. It did help, I guess, but the best answer would have been just obedience. Everything was God's doing, and I'm simply made to obey and be a vessel of His goodness. When we own something as our doing, we take the glory away from God. But if you think long and hard, is pregnancy a product of human hands or God's?

Days into the pregnancy, thoughts of miscarriage paralyzed me. I remembered three of my friend's stories and feared my own. But as usual, God is patient. He waited until I realized the cause of my fear — owning the glory of the pregnancy. He reminded me of His promises. I let go and let Him. God always knows best for Unyara and me. Worrying was killing the joy out of the experience, but not for long.

Since I was young, God has always been there for me, but I have always put Him in the friend zone. Once I learned that God is speaking to us every day, sending us little hints of His love that often goes not responded because we were too busy with the wrong things, my heart just changed. Reading Godly posts no longer sends shivers to my spine. The miracles in my life have started melting the darkness within. Showing my love and gratefulness to God is not excellent in a generation of too much idolatry but compared to who I was before, this time, I only care about one thing. God's thought about me. I am what God thinks I am. It's much easier to say that we got pregnant because we did something humanly than saying God opened our womb for the child to grow, like how God opened Rachel's womb after long years of barrenness.

Then God remembered Rachel, and God listened to her and opened her womb. And she conceived and bore a son and said, "God has taken away my reproach."

But no matter how we rehash the events of how Unyara came to be, nothing is in our hands; everything is in God's hands. I remembered how I started twenty-eighteen with zero thoughts of a baby already. I accepted that God might have other plans for me, as the baby didn't come in twenty-seventeen as prayed. When I made my yearly resolution, I just wrapped twenty-seventeen on a list and didn't make any big plans for twenty-eighteen. I thought that it was because I have already developed conscious mindfulness to not sweat on the small stuff, especially self-imposed one.

When we discovered the pregnancy in February of twenty-eighteen, my first thought was an aha moment. God purposely let me be flexible at twenty-eighteen because He was cooking up something better. Twenty-seventeen was a mix of everything. I didn't have specific resolutions, but I focused on stopping being who I usually am. The husband said that my subconscious desire to make each year awesome than the passing year is draining. It's only a matter of time before it takes a toll. So, in twenty-eighteen, I continued what I started in twenty-seventeen and just stopped being what I usually am. I let God drive and listen to my husband more. I focus on completing my #Bible365 daily devotional. With less Facebook, I had more daily entries on my gratitude and prayer journal. We ticked our goal board at a relaxed pace. Gone are the days of complaining about downtimes. I appreciate un-busy days and connect with more people face to face. I developed a listening ear and tried to be more informed on what's happening globally. In the continued reading of productive stuff, I learned how to be a godly wife. Read more on how to balance being a Christian. Most of all — learn to listen to God's voice. The things that I embraced in twenty-eighteen were things that have helped me during the pregnancy.

The last post on my blog before the cryptic pregnancy announcement was a narration of how crazy the starting days of twenty-eighteen have been. We are often blinded by the tests that we forgot how it could become a testimony. We focus on the problem that it magnifies even more significant than God. Everyday disputes can turn into a full-blown battle if we are not careful with our actions. Pure kindness can be colored with ulterior motives with the wrong recipient—trivial things to a scandal in a toxic environment. Every day, we are faced with tests that will challenge our faith and trust in Christ. We encounter people who will make us stumble and question our faith in God's choices. As we fight the everyday worldly battle of staying afloat as a child of God, we get discouraged and may question our worth and our place in His kingdom. January was tough spiritually. I felt barren and dried up. The husband and I got into arguments about almost anything. I was Miss Sunshine on the outside, but there was darkness within. I was having a hard time reigniting my passion for the Lord. Going back to the power of talking to God and drawing strength from Him instead of my own was ultimately off the bat.

After countless personal pushes of finding my passion with Him, I failed. The spiritual evolved into physical sickness. I have come to loathe the idea of continuing to serve. Suddenly, everything was more complicated than it usually is. Tired and out of options, I resort to the idea of quitting. It was the only way at first, but after connecting with my ministry again and the counsel of Godly sisters,

I saw God's hand reaching out to me. I was not alone. I just thought I was.

When I knew about the pregnancy, the crazy moods at the start of the year made more sense. Overwhelming happiness then anxiousness and fear and vice versa. There was a mixture of emotions since God revealed the miracle. All I could think was to share with the world how God finally answered our prayers. I couldn't recall how many times I have paused and pondered if it was real. Tears would involuntarily fall upon realizing just how much of a miracle it was. I couldn't keep thanking Him. There were highs. Then comes the fear, paralyzing what-ifs and crippling anxiousness. But God was there all the way. He was faithfully listening to my woes and worries. He kept reassuring me of His promise.

Dearest Kring, you have been holding on to me for the longest time, do not let go now when you need me the most. Please do not be anxious about anything, for my purpose is more significant than your worries. Keep trusting and believing in me. This will be a hard time, but because you are my beloved, you will not be alone. We are in this together. Your success is my success. Your test is my test. I will be with you all the way, dearest Kring. You and your passenger will always be covered with my love and guidance.

The worries didn't last long. God assured me that

no matter what happens, He will look after us. Unyara was His miracle. He owns it. No matter what I do, His will comes first. Realizing that I am only an instrument of His grand plan calmed my raging, anxious heart. The Lord is in control. When the Lord is in control, all things are possible, even growing a seed in barren soil.

Before I had Unyara, I thought when you get pregnant, everything just flows. What I learned is that pregnancy is just the start. There is so much that could happen during the nine months. Surviving the first trimester is a miracle too.

We discovered that Unyara was aboard on the seventeenth of February twenty-eighteen via a one-time test of a Home Pregnancy Test Kit. Since it was Saturday, I went to a center for a Transvaginal Ultrasound to confirm. I was six weeks pregnant, but it was still a gestational sac. No embryo has grown yet. It was also our church's couple ministry's first meetup. That's when I realized how God just keeps sending me love letters through dates and lumping life's milestones together. Now every time we attend our couple's ministry's anniversary, we would remember that as an anniversary of Unyara's pregnancy too.

Suffering from polycystic ovarian syndrome since twenty-ten and being heartbroken in August twenty-seventeen after drinking pills for eight months, the pregnancy is indeed a miracle and an answered prayer. We might have been married for three years now, but it was only at twenty-seventeen that we desired a baby. And God being the outstanding God He is and always faithful to His promises, He gave us His miracle. And ever since that day of the discovery, I can feel God's guidance throughout, reminding and reassuring me every time how His ways are higher than mine.

Because I transferred to a new job on September twenty-seventeen, it changed my health coverage. I didn't know any obstetricians at my new insurance company. By God's grace, a friend from the office recommended a name which was the obstetrician on duty on the day I visited. On our first meeting, I was requested for laboratories, and it looked like I had a Urinary Tract Infection. It was the first scare of my pregnancy.

On my first transvaginal ultrasound, I was told for a repeat procedure after two weeks to check if the embryo has grown and for the heartbeat at eight weeks. The days leading to the day of the ultrasound were another anxiety struggle. On my first transvaginal ultrasound, I knew a friend. When I saw her again while waiting for my turn, she shared her miscarriage. My heart went out to her and realized how unstable pregnancies could be. If not for the husband who was there with me, I would have cried aloud. I felt her pain. When it was finally three turns before me, I heard the women's results before me. My sadness increased listening to their sad results. And as if knowing my pain, the husband kept entertaining me with his antics as I busied myself reading God's words.

When it was finally our turn, the husband went with me. When the doctor said that the baby has grown with good cardiac activity, relief overtook me. I went to the comfort room after and let out a cry of gratitude. God is so good indeed. And I wondered how an eight-week baby could bring so much joy and sadness at the same time. It was then that I realized that being pregnant is only a start. There's still so much to experience and trials that may come with the pregnancy. We would indeed not survive on our own. We need God every step of the way.

The threat of a urinary tract infection cut the happiness of the baby's heartbeat. Back in the twenty-ten, due to my unusual pee habits and workaholism, I was confined due to a urinary tract infection. It was okay as I wasn't pregnant, but having a urinary tract infection, especially in the first trimester, poses a threat to our little one. Worsening the matter, I also had a sore throat and fever. The obstetrician explained that it might be because of the bacteria. I was prescribed antibiotics and told to hope that the infection would respond to the medicine or face a much bigger problem.

The following days were a cycle of over-drinking water, cranberry juices, and countable com-

WHEN NOTHING FEELS RIGHT AT THIRTY-FIVE | 153

fort room trips. It was such a hassle, but what comforted me was the lack of pregnancy nausea and other common pregnancy woes. Because we have a family trip during the weekend, I had to go checkup early. Praise God for my flexible work arrangement; I was able to work while waiting for my lab results and appointment. Thankfully, the prayers and lifestyle adjustment worked. I was cleared of the infection and was told that the next meeting would be to check the baby's heartbeat via doppler on my fifth prenatal checkup.

Days prior, I was on an anxiety attack again. All sorts of paranoia run in my head. Thankfully, reading bible devotionals gets me out of misery. I reminded myself that God is in control. Worrying with my human strength is useless. No matter what happens, God has the last say. It also helped that every night, the husband and I prayed together for the baby's health and standard delivery.

However, a day earlier, before the scheduled checkup, I had an allergy. I can't sleep well because of it. Unfortunately, the obstetrician had an emergency, so we were rescheduled. When we return, the baby's heartbeat is good, but only the obstetrician could hear it so far. I'm also advised to work at home for a week to cure my allergy.

What I learned from the first trimester of my pregnancy is that we are God guarded. God is faithful in His promises. Day by day, He has assured me of

His love and guidance. When we knew about the pregnancy at six weeks, I expected to have famed nausea and vomiting; to my disappointment, I had none. Thanks to my husband and some friends, I realized that every woman's pregnancy journey is different. I should be thankful that I'm one of those blessed few who were spared the hassle. What didn't manifest as pregnancy symptoms come out as a baby bump as early as eight weeks? I received comments about the size of my belly. It bothers me at first, but in the end, I realized that people say what they want to say, but it doesn't mean that it's meant for you to take it to heart. If you know what's happening and you are happy with how you look, people's comments should remain as comments.

Expecting a baby is our most excellent adventure. We might have trekked to a few summits and traveled in and outside the Philippines, but raising a baby takes more than strength. Our mental capacity gained from playing several board games would even cut. We may have organized our wedding, mortgaged, and managed our condo rental business, but this is the first time that we received a gift that we thought that only a miracle could. Not sure if the things that we learn prior can be applied. Wonder if excel of itineraries, budgeting, and schedules could keep us grounded in our goals and remind us constantly of the purpose of this blessing.

Months passed, and its gender reveal: Is it Gani or Yara? Internet signs point to Gani, but more friends are going for Yara. For us, it doesn't matter whether Baby Love is Izaya Isagani or Unyara Teresa. We are praying for Baby Love to be healthy in all areas. At the height of my hate of having a baby, I gave up the right to name our child years ago. I honor the agreement, so the husband was in charge. He preferred names that are Bisaya-spelled and unique. Among the baby names for both genders: Unyara Seresa (Yara) and Izaya Isagani (Gani) emerged as the winners. Teresa is the Bisaya term for Cherry, while Izaya is a different spelling of the Biblical name-Isaiah. When the husband's niece from Canada visited last March, she looked up the name Yara and shared that it means little butterfly in some language. What a way to name our first baby girl, indeed.

We planned a gender shoot on the first weekend of June, but due to conflicts, we turned it into a recorded gender reveal. The husband suggested that our do-it-yourself video could include our reaction, so we must tell the sonographer to put the gender result on a sealed envelope instead of announcing it on the spot.

Aside from the gender reveal, I have many celebratory plans in mind before pregnancy, but after my readings, I realized that some of them are just vanity and pompousness. Who in their right mind would think of three different parties to celebrate? I did. I thought of a gender reveal, a baby shower, and a welcome party. My thirty-second birthday party wasn't even part of the three parties I was supposed to splurge on. So technically, four parties!

When I shared it with my husband, he gave me a look. I know very well what it meant. If I were the same Kresia back then, I would have ignored that look and do what I want. So, I reluctantly settled with one. Even that one party was questionable to him. Why the need to organize a party on my own was beyond him. Of course, it seems like not organizing a party was a problem, but now, I don't think it is. Instead of spending money on the party, I could buy the stuff we need. In this age of parties for a gender reveal, baby showers, and welcome parties, it's a different story not to have any.

Spending my thirty-second birthday with Unyara aboard at thirty-two weeks was perfection. It is nice to be celebrating it at a party but spending it low-key wouldn't lower the value of the awesomeness of God's plan. It's just my pride and vanity who wants it grand. And besides, I miss my friends too. The party would have been a perfect venue to reconnect, but as the husband points out, would I have the time to do that considering the number of people I'm friends with? Even the final guest list is a headache. Do I want to go through that hassle of selecting the top fifty of my best friends again, just like what I did at our wedding? Now that I remember it, I hurt some because they weren't on the list.

There's a reason why baby showers are small and intimate gatherings because it is a venue where the attendees could talk to the mom or dad about the new journey. What I planned to do is not have a baby shower at all. It's a bit sad not to pursue what I plan to do, but I will live through it. From the start, the mind shift that I went through since Unyara arrived has always been fascinating.

Financial readiness is one of the many considerations about pregnancy. We weren't lacking, but we know we may sacrifice some things for Unyara. When we decided to prepare for Unyara in twenty-seventeen, we thought what we had been enough. But God felt differently. Provision coming before a vision is God's promise. But it is not suitable to be spending mindlessly because God has been generously providing us with what we need.

Instead of an elaborate party for my thirty-second birthday, I gathered six of my girlfriends for a maternity shoot at our condo. God was super wonderful, too, because one of my sisters in Christ is also pregnant. We even have the same due date. It was super remarkable to be celebrating the milestone together. Having someone to share the pregnancy journey is what I have dreamed of. I wanted to do that with my elementary best friend, but even if it didn't happen to her, I'm super blessed to have it with another. Aside from the girlfriend maternity shoot, God made the maternity shoot with the husband occurred too. Considering the husband's character, I never thought it would.

For the first trimester of pregnancy, one of my significant realizations was that no pregnancy is ever the same. No amount of reading and interviewing mothers can prepare you for what's about to come. In the second trimester, God removed all the anxiety. There's just peace and trust in God more. It feels shorter than the first trimester, even though it's technically longer. Throughout the pregnancy, we didn't stop our activities. We kicked off the second trimester in Pinamungajan for my team building. Because it was summer, there were back-to-back escapes, and we enjoyed all of them because, like the first trimester, the chill pregnancy continues. The only clue that I'm pregnant is my bulging tummy. All others were the same. There were hiccups here and there, but nothing major. I deactivated my Facebook starting the first of May twenty eighteen, on the fourth month of my pregnancy, so I updated less in social media for most of my second trimester. The sabbatical may have helped because by not sharing as much, I have spared myself from feedback. But that didn't stop those who were in contact with me from imposing their beliefs as to how I should take care of myself and my pregnancy as if they are experts in the field. I got over it too and learned not to mind because I know what I'm doing, and I'm confident that most of what they are saying speaks much of themselves than with my circumstances. And they love me as well. To keep me at peace, every prenatal, I record my weight, and other stats then note the significant highlights.

At week fifteen, I had my first tummy ultrasound and hoped I'd know the gender. Of course, it was too early, but we discovered something important — I had a low-lying placenta. If not for my excitement, we wouldn't have known about it. In the first trimester, I'd get very anxious when making love, fearing it might affect the baby. The assurances of my obstetrician and the articles were not enough to appease me. I preferred not to deprive the husband of his rights, but I was too anxious. The husband understood my anxiety and was ultra-supportive. When my obstetrician knew about the low-lying placenta, we were told to abstain. I told her we already did. It was a good call because only God knows what could have happened if I didn't listen to my instinct and the husband didn't honor my anxiety.

At week twenty, my obstetrician changes her mind on the congenital anomaly scan schedule. I was heartbroken because I was excited to know the gender. When I left the obstetrician, I was just down, and without really thinking much about it, I found myself at another center asking for the ultrasound schedule. It was already four in the afternoon, so I didn't know there's an available slot. Good thing it has. I went ahead and had the gender checked. I reminded the obstetrician not to tell me directly but to seal it in an envelope instead so the husband and I would know the gender together.

To celebrate the pregnancy, I planned parties, but as the month progresses, so are my views on pompous celebrations. I scrapped every party idea and used the money to buy major items for Unyara. I just created a gender reveal video instead. It's not much, but it gets the job done without spending as much.

Every week I often assess myself against the expected discomfort because I wanted to be ready if it happened. In the second trimester, I was prepared for the back pains, insomnia, and all other aches, but in the first trimester, there were none. At the end of the second trimester, I had nerve pains and a diabetes scare. It was nothing major. My sugar just spiked because I had been munching on sweets, which were very unusual since I got pregnant. I was only ordered to limit sweets and monitor my ring finger. The results were negative for diabetes, though, but now and then, I get anxious when I crave something sweet. The second trimester passed by so quickly. What they say about the second trimester being the honeymoon stage of pregnancy is very accurate.

At thirty weeks, on my seventh week in the third trimester, I was down due to colds, headache, and tonsillitis. I had a urinary tract infection scare too, so I had to visit my obstetrician unplanned. A urinary tract infection does not cause fever because I had few bacteria in my blood. I was ordered to rest and have plenty of water. No meds. But I was asked to eat, sleep and monitor my temperature. We were supposed to attend the board gaming event one Saturday night, but since I was sick, the husband and I missed the fun. Thankfully, my fever went down around midnight. It came back this morning, but after a lukewarm bath, apple cider gargle, and garlic candy, my tonsillitis and fever subsided. The craze hasn't come back, but my nose is still stuffy, and I have a cough. I was feeling a little lightheaded still but feeling better. I may have pushed myself a little hard from all the pregnancy nesting and processing the papers to get our condo bond. Pregnancy didn't change my wonder woman's feels of having no internal limit to what it can do. Most of the time, I'll only know I've had enough when my body screams enough.

At week thirty-three, I was already looking forward to four more weeks of pregnancy. The earlier, the better. Upon reading, I'm officially ripe for popping at week thirty-seven on the twenty-second of September. Even if my due date is the thirteenth of October, I didn't lounge around but started doing the prepping at week thirty-seven. September is officially off-limits to anything but preparations. We opened September, one in a labor class and another by the fifteenth of September. Despite the advice to work at home early by my colleagues, I am still in the office on Wednesdays and continue taking the stairs and walking. My initial maternity date was a day before my due date. A friend from work called me crazy. And as a person who likes to start things at the end of the month, when she suggested that it might be best to start maternity by the start of October, I agreed. Reluctant but listened as the extra time to exercise is tempting. Thanks to that friend because Unyara was born seven days earlier than my actual due date.

"Oi, ka gwapa gud nimo. Red lips man kau ka and white." Said the still groggy me at the operating room when the pedia had her latch on me. In my mind was a picture of snow-white. Cool. She is worth every pain indeed.

I ended at the operating room after twelve hours of normal labor on the sixth of October twenty-eighteen. It was my first humbling moment when Unyara arrived. Very proud of how easy my pregnancy was. I thought that normal labor was a breeze, but God had a different plan.

I had an early obstetrician checkup on the fourth of October instead of the scheduled sixth of October because I panicked when I didn't notice Unyara moved. Since week thirty-seven, paranoia has been my constant woe. I was hearing and reading stories of babies dying because of cord coil and other causes before delivery was heartbreaking and making me paranoid. I want Unyara out as soon as possible. It doesn't help that on our latest ultrasound at Week thirty-six, she has one cord coil on her neck, so when I noticed a difference on Thursday, I had to do something to the husband's surprise. I reasoned that I was worried because she didn't move, but after drinking a glass of raspberry iced tea, she did, but I still pursued the ultrasound to the husband's disapproving stare. Well, eight hundred pesos is worth something, but I didn't mind. I need to make sure she is alright. I thought the short side trip before a late lunch date would end early, so I had to cancel the meeting with my friend. It wasn't a wasted trip, though, because I found out, Unyara now has two cord coils. Her weight increases from the last ultrasound. Since I was in the vicinity, the obstetrician continued the checkup. When I arrived, the clinic entertained me right away, as it was surprisingly less crowded. I shared my ordeal with the obstetrician. To appease both of us, I was told to go to my assigned hospital to have a Non-Stress Test to check if Unyara's movement is expected.

The procedure was supposed to be done at the emergency room, but because it was jam-packed at six in the evening, I was forwarded to the delivery room instead. I was happy because I will get a glimpse of my future room. Surprise blessing! The test returned well. Unyara's movement was excellent, and we also found out that I have contractions already. Still, I told the resident obstetrician that I was only one cm per my last internal exam that afternoon. I am not in pain and have no contractions. When I left, I bid them goodbye saying, see you in a week perhaps; I was unaware that it would be sooner than I expected.

I woke up at six o'clock in the morning of the fifth of October because of dysmenorrhea pain radiating from my lower back to my tummy. It was a first, so I was happy to realize it must have been some contractions because I can already feel it despite my high tolerance to pain. I told the husband casually; there was no urgency because, as of yesterday's early obstetrician checkup, I'm still at one cm. The husband and I were at odds in the morning cause despite the contractions, I felt it would be better not to change the day's activities. When my mother-in-law knew about my contractions and how I'm feeling, she said that I shouldn't walk all alone and suggested that the husband should accompany me. But the husband has to work, so he wanted me to be in the house, but I didn't see the urgency of the situation. After an altercation, we ended up doing my plan for the day, and to my remorse, he insisted on keeping me company. We dropped by the condo first. Due to traffic back and forth, we arrived at our next stop, the clinic, to check my contractions. After lining up, we had lunch and returned to the house for a quick nap. Before I returned to the obstetrician, the husband went to work. It was already three o'clock in the afternoon when we went back, so I just asked him to accompany me to see the obstetrician instead. It was a good call because when I was checked, I was already four centimeters. Usually, by three centimeters, you will be sent for the hospital admission. Because it was almost dinner time, we decided to do errands first. The husband asked me if I was okay. I figured that I don't want to wait in the hospital to take our time. We withdrew money and went to the house for dinner. We arrived at the hospital around seven o'clock in the evening. After the assessment at emergency, I was placed in the labor room. The husband and mother-in-law stayed in the room.

Despite the two cord coils, I was positive that standard delivery is possible considering my superwoman health and strength. It took me twelve hours+, two different bedmates, and an over-the-top agony that knows no end to give up the dream of standard delivery. Today, I have a different look at mothers. Labor is painful even to my high tolerance of pain. I'm thankful for the videos and friends' suggestions; I have managed to get through nine cm of normal labor without tears and no shouting. Grateful to the staff and resident obstetrician for being very supportive. Their travel chitchats have kept me company.

Four hours have elapsed, but there was no change with my four centimeters opening. The contractions get stronger by then, and the pain was horrendous. I kept my poise by thinking this too shall pass. I was told that from that point forward, the internal check would be done every two to four hours, depending on the contractions. That has been my ray of light. I kept looking forward to internal check time, even if it's annoyingly painful because it's the only way to know if I have made progress.

By eleven o'clock, I progressed to six, and my water broke. It was also when my first bedmate, who has been there for two nights, finally concluded to have a cesarean. Her progress has been plodding, even if her water broke already. It was a little family ruckus. Her attending obstetrician wanted the resident obstetrician to scrub with her, but since I went into active labor too, she suggested having another obstetrician scrub. The labor room went silent when my bedmate left. We only exchanged a little story because rest is a priority after my active labor.

At around four a.m., I progressed to eight cm. It was also when a new bedmate had arrived, occupying the space of the one who left. She was already seven cm and was carrying a boy, like my first bedmate. Because the pain was crazy by this time, socializing was out of the window. She was the one who smiled first. She's a year older than me, unlike the first, who is five years my junior. At seven cm, her water didn't break yet. Mine broke at seven cm, and I was already at eight. I was technically ahead. When my obstetrician arrived around six o'clock in the morning, I was told to push during contractions because on the last internal checkup finally; I was already a nine. However, Unyara is still high up. She needed to come down for head crowning. While I was busy doing my thing, my bedmate suddenly screamed around seven o'clock in the morning. The top of the head of her baby is already out. We were shocked. It was such a fast transition. Comparing the first and the second bedmates' progress, I was already considering an opt-out of the pain. I had the two cord coils considered too. By eight, I draw the line. I was already exhausted from pushing. Yet still no progress on Unyara's end. An apparatus monitored Unyara's heartbeat throughout the pushes because of the two cord coils. However, there was no sign that she is distressed. I decided to do a cesarean after calling the husband and got his yes.

I was happy to have been out of the labor pain misery, but when the idea of the cesarean procedure dawned on me, I got a bit scared. This would be my first time on the operating table. Throughout my ordeal in labor pains, God was with me. I kept asking Him to take me out of the agony, and maybe it was tearless because God makes it less painful. He gave me enough to appreciate motherhood and enough to keep me sane. But at the operating table, I surrendered my life to Him. I'm not a fan of medicines and medical procedures because I always want what's natural, but at that time, I had no choice. I could continue pushing at Unyara's expense because I want to avoid being in the operating room. But as a mother, would it be the right call? I have done my best already by enduring the labor pains, even if they ended in the operating room. Instead of feeling sad, I feel victorious and accomplished because I was able to experience the labor pains. It would have been nice to see it through the end, but the journey alone has convinced me that I am better off spending than going through that one again. Labor pains will be different each time, but I prefer not to subject myself to that anymore.

On the operating procedure, the contractions didn't subside. I was told not to move because the anesthesia will be injected into my spine. I prayed that I wouldn't move or else I'd endanger myself. Thank God that the anesthesiologist injected the anesthesia successfully. In minutes, it numbed my pain. I was also told I'd be given sedatives, but I was awake the entire time. I talked a lot and was told to stop talking since it will make me vomit. Not only that, but I was even on a minimized talk policy. It's so hard.

Before the procedure, I asked the obstetrician to take a picture of Unyara. I forgot that they would be the ones to do the finishing. Good thing the anesthesiologist took pictures too. Super grateful to them who captured the moment. Unyara saw the world on the sixth of October twenty-eighteen at ten in the morning. After the procedure, I was transferred to a recovery room. By two in the afternoon, I was assigned to my room. Unyara is still in the nursery so that I can recover first. My delivery story is an incredible journey. I don't want it another way. I'm happy to note that Unyara picked a great birthdate. My last menstrual flow is on the sixth of January. She was born on the sixth of October. God has times our call to cesarian, too. Had I pursued the standard delivery, she would have defecated inside me, which can cause complications. She was pulled out in time. She defecated immediately after she is out of my tummy.

Unyara was born a day before my mom's birthday. I only realized the significance of that as I was writing. Understanding my mom was not my best asset. We have a complicated relationship. I blamed her for all my bad character. She has broken me beyond repair that I never dreamed of having a child of my own. But when Unyara was born, it felt like I was given a new hope to save myself by becoming the mother I never had. I can't change the past, but I have the chance to change my future. For that alone, my thirty-five years in this world are worth living. I am sincerely anticipating my next memoirs on motherhood. While waiting for that, here's to praying that what you have learned from my life will be a guiding light to your own. May you have a faith-filled life centered in Jesus too!

EPILOGUE

Dearest 45-year-old-Kring,

You have come a long way since you released this book on your 35th birthday. Whatever your reason for picking up this book again, know that this too shall pass. You may have reached a slump, feel stuck, unmotivated and nothing feels right at 45, but know that this is just all a feeling. You have been this way before. All you have to do is trust in God's promise (Romans 8:28).

> **And we know that in all things God works for the good of those who love him, who have been called according to his purpose.**

Go to your nook and connect with God to lead you where you should be. God bless you always, Kring. You are blessed and favored. Do not forget your purpose.

With love of lots,
35-year-old-Kring

ACKNOWLEDGEMENT

My heartfelt gratitude to God for the idea and for giving me the strength and bravery to pursue my dream. And to all my families and friends who have inspired and encouraged me.

To Mama Sepen. You may never know and understand the weight of what's written here, but know that despite all the struggles that I had, I am grateful that you are my Mom. It is my prayer that you can snap out of your bipolar and come back to us. We've come a long way, Ma. It is sad that you can't fully enjoy the fruits of your labor because of your mental condition, but we can only do so much. I hope to one day sit with you and share with you the stories here. Some may be hard for you and me, but I won't care as long as you are back with us.

To Dodong Gigil. Thank you Dong for being a big part of why I could break free from the family responsibility. Sometimes, I feel guilty for leaving you behind, but there was never a time that you questioned my decision. I am so happy with what you have become. I hope you know that I'm still your number one fan. Whenever you encourage me, I feel happy because I never really thought that one day our roles would be reversed. I'm so proud of you, Dong. You are one of God's blessings to me. Whenever I ponder on how far you have gone, my pains are justified. Continue to inspire us, Dong. Thank you for the love and dedication to the family. And for always remembering me in your victories and travels.

To Migo. Words are not your love language. You may not appreciate what I will write, so I will keep it short. Thank you for being the superman behind. I know you find it hard to understand since I am complicated, but always know that I am better because of you. Your character always reminded me of Jesus. No matter how complicated I am, you always find reasons to stick with me. Thank you for the love, Migo. I won't promise anything, but know that I am trying my best every day to be half of who you are in character. Excited to be spending the rest of our life together where you will get annoyed by my "old" stories. Haha!

To Unyara. I don't know where to begin, but let me start with "I love you". I can't wait for you to grow up to understand the things that are written here. You are the product of faith, Baby Love! My heart is overwhelmed with love and admiration for who you are. Every day I am learning a lot about becoming a mother that you need. As you grow, please guide me to support you and to assert what you want. Don't let me become the mother that I hated.

I love you so much. You are God's love in the flesh!

To Velou and Thelma. Thank you for being here. I didn't plan for any of you to stay with us, but God knows me best indeed. Having both of you in the house has made things better. I have never seen Unyara warm up to anyone other than me. Also, taking out cooking every day has given me time to do something else.

To Fatima and Jackie. Thank you for taking care of Casamira construction. I had the time to write the chapters of the book because of it.

To Analyn. Thank you for encouraging me to pursue the outrageous thought and even send a link for writing your own book. I appreciate it so much.

To Corie and Grace. Thank you for volunteering to be the first reader.

To Charina and Joy. Thank you for asking about the book's progress. It makes me happy.

To Charry and Dena. Thank you for reading my chats about the book.

To Gams. Thank you for encouraging me through IG posts.

To Leonila, Brooke, Thelma, Ana Maria and Cams. Thank you for reacting to my FIRST BOOK UPDATE on Facebook. Your reaction made my day and feel less alone.

To Precious and Jill. Thank you for encouraging me via a comment on my SECOND BOOK UPDATE on Facebook. Your comment has become an inspiration.

To Vien, Anette, Thelma, Jessica and Francis Charlene. Thank you for reacting to my SECOND BOOK UPDATE on Facebook. Your reaction made my day and feel inspired.

To Mommy Lucring. Thank you for encouraging me via a comment on my THIRD BOOK UPDATE on Facebook. Your comment has become an inspiration.

To the new reactors of my THIRD BOOK UPDATE on Facebook (Mary Jane, Charina, Leah, Perpetua, Antonio, Bula, Rayshell, Pam, Te Amay, Mae, Belle, Glenn, Ruth, Flora, Devina, Katrina, Marj, John2, Divine, Melody, Carmela, Retchell, Charlyn, Baby Fatima, Marichu, Yra, Dean, Quoyniegay). Thank you for your interaction. It made me happy!

To the new reactors of my FOURTH BOOK UPDATE on Facebook (Nona, Gretchen, Norms, Rufamae, Michelle Dan, Maria). Thank you for your interaction. It made me happy!

Advance thank you to everyone who will read the book especially to those who will provide feedback of improvements. Connect with me through instagram: #WNFRa35

ABOUT THE AUTHOR

Kring July

She is a woman of style whose fashion would make you doubt the validity of her stories in conquering mountains. She is a software engineer by profession since 2007, fitness buff, DIY fan, Airbnb host from 2014 to 2020, mom to a toddler, and Jesus lover. Her hobbies include writing, blogging, scrap/photo booking, traveling, trekking and volunteering. In 2016, Kring has contributed 2 posts in Tripzilla.ph about "Backpacking in Indochina". She shares her everyday life at "lifewithkring.wordpress.com". In 2020, she had psoriasis and launched "lifewithpsor.wordpress.com" to document the journey. Kring's old writings can be read at "kringwrote.wordpress.com". Born and raised in Cebu, Philippines, Kring July is married to an introvert who understands and supports her OVERLY extrovert personality. She became a mother to Unyara on October 2018.

Made in the USA
Las Vegas, NV
04 June 2024